BASIC VALUES
AND
ETHICAL DECISIONS

BASIC VALUES
AND
ETHICAL DECISIONS:

An Examination of Individualism and Community in American Society

---

by
GERRY C. HEARD

ROBERT E. KRIEGER PUBLISHING COMPANY
MALABAR, FLORIDA
1990

Original Edition 1990

Printed and Published by
ROBERT E. KRIEGER PUBLISHING COMPANY, INC.
KRIEGER DRIVE
MALABAR, FL 32950

Copyright © 1990 by Robert E. Krieger Publishing Co., Inc.

Library of Congress Cataloging-in-Publication Data

Heard, Gerry C.
    Basic values and ethical decisions: an examination of
individualism and community in American society / Gerry C. Heard.
        p. cm.
    ISBN 0-89464-431-9
    1. Individualism. 2. Community. 3. Value. 4. Decision-Making
(Ethics) 5. Social ethics. 6. United States—Moral conditions.
    7. United States—Social conditions—1980–   I. Title.
B824.H43 1990
302.5'4'0973—dc20   89-27530
                                                          CIP

10   9   8   7   6   5   4   3   2

Dedicated to
Granville, Lorene, Donna, Leslie, and Jana
for their companionship and encouragement over the years

Acknowledgments

There have been a number of people who have assisted me while I was writing this book, and at this point I would like to express my appreciation for their contributions. These include certain families who offered substantial amounts of financial aid to Louisiana College which allowed me opportunities for research and writing during sabbatical programs. These are Mr. and Mrs. C. O. Walker and Mr. and Mrs. Andrew Walker for their grant to faculty development as well as Dr. and Mrs. John H. Colvin for their gift to the Department of Religion and Philosophy. Others to whom I am grateful are Dr. Norman Bowie of the University of Delaware and Dr. Bill Cooper of Baylor University for their friendship and help while I worked at their institutions. I also appreciate the efforts of Kathi Franklin and Carol L. Beeman who did the typing for the first manuscript.

In addition, I am especially thankful to my parents, Granville and Lorene, and to my wife, Donna, and my children, Leslie and Jana. They have provided me with an abundance of love and support during my work, and it is to them that this book is dedicated.

Gerry C. Heard
Louisiana College

CONTENTS

INTRODUCTION

Our values are the concepts in life that we appreciate and which we accept and allow to become a part of who we are. They serve as standards for how we understand ourselves and the world around us, and we often use them as a basis for our decisions and actions. These values can be divided into a number of different types such as moral, religious, social, or aesthetic in nature, but they also can be distinguished in terms of the degree of significance that we ascribe to them. Some of our values are strongly held as may be the case with moral and religious values, whereas other values are given a low priority such as may be the case with a subjective preference like a favorite color.

However, one's value system does not exist in a state of complete harmony. Some of our values are in tension with each other in the sense that conflicts may arise between them. In some cases these value conflicts are such that decisions have to be made in a given situation about which value will be given priority. For instance, a person may have to decide how to use leisure time such as whether to watch television or go out with the family. Both practices may be valued, but both cannot be carried out at the same time. In other cases the opposition between values may not be that priority has to be decided according to the circumstances. It may be necessary to emphasize both values at all times, but the tension between them makes this difficult to accomplish. This kind of tension can exist, for example, between valuing the friendship of others and keeping a sense of self-respect. One may want and also need the acceptance of others, at least to some extent, and at the same time desire to maintain a high degree of personal integrity. Sometimes a problem arises in being able to have both of these simultaneously.

Individualism and community are two broad and influential values in American experience which exist in tension with each other. The tension between them resembles more the latter type of conflict that has been mentioned. Each of these notions contains values which most people would regard as worthy, and, consequently, they would want to include both of them in their lives to some degree. No doubt circumstances exist in which choices have to be made between them, but overall it is more a matter of determining how they interact and how both can be affirmed together. But how can such an approach best be accomplished? In what way can individualism and community be joined into a constructive life-style? The purpose of this book is to answer this question. It carefully examines individualism and community in order to acquire a more rewarding understanding of their meaning and relationship.

To achieve this purpose, the book first discusses in Chapter 1 the various expressions of individualism and community in the American past as well as the ways that these concepts manifest themselves in contemporary American society. This chapter also points to the tension between these notions that was present in the past and continues to be present today. The book then turns in Chapters 2, 3, 4, and 5 to an analysis of some specific value conflicts growing out of the tension between individualism and community. These include the conflicts of achievement and benevolence, private interests and the public good, detachment and involvement, and independence and dependence. In each case the conflict is explained and a means of reconciling it is suggested. Then finally in Chapter 6 the work looks again at the general concepts of individualism and community and recommends new ways of understanding them in the future. It also makes practical suggestions about how these new approaches can be attained by an individual.

This book seeks to provide a realistic and honest assessment of the American situation. Even though it recognizes that American society continues to maintain many positive attributes, it often draws attention to the dark side of the American experience. It frequently points to problems within society and weaknesses in traditional values in an effort to encourage social improvements and personal growth.

Also, this book is designed to be used for instruction in the classroom. It includes discussion questions and suggested readings at the end of each chapter and additionally provides case studies for consideration at the end of Chapters 2, 3, 4, and 5. Although the persons and details in these cases are fictional, they were written to portray the real life dilemmas resulting from the tension between individualism and community.

CHAPTER 1

THE AMERICAN HERITAGE OF
INDIVIDUALISM AND COMMUNITY

The notions of individualism and community indicate two contrasting sets of values in American society. On the one hand, individualism provides a perspective upon human nature in terms of the way people exist by themselves with only incidental references being made to others. It focuses upon the human condition as it exists apart from others and serves to promote ideas of personal freedom, self-improvement, privacy, achievement, independence, detachment, and self-interests. Although the exercise of these individualistic concepts may result in the person's having contact with others, this interaction is not an essential aspect of their meaning. Their essential meaning concerns the rights and needs that people have on their own and separate from their relationships with others.

On the other hand, community sets forth a view of people within the context of human relationships. It concentrates on qualities that people have through their associations with others such as intimacy, benevolence, fellowship, belonging, dependence, social involvement, and the public good. Of course, the term "community" is sometimes used to refer to a location, but in this discussion it will be thought of, like individualism, as primarily an outlook that includes certain values. However, unlike individualism, the approach of community emphasizes the significance that a network of relationships has for a person's life. It gives attention to that side of the self that calls for an acknowledgment of others and the part that they play in one's existence.

This chapter offers a further explanation of individualism and community by examining their existence in American society in both the past and the present. It discusses the American heritage of these notions and then looks at some examples of them in our society today. It also points out that a certain amount of tension exists between these concepts as Americans seek to make value choices.

THE HERITAGE OF INDIVIDUALISM

Two types of individualism that have been a part of American society since its beginning are economic and political. These developed together in American thought in the seventeenth and eighteenth centuries and have much in common. Both emphasized individual liberty in their particular domains of society. Economic individualism asserted the value of a spontaneous economic system based on the right of private property and also individual freedom in production, exchange, and competitive efforts. It claimed that this type of economy is self-adjusting and most conducive to the satisfaction of individuals and the welfare of society. Political individualism stressed that political authority should lie in the will and purposes of the individuals in society. The people should have the freedom to govern themselves by means of majority rule, and it is a responsibility of government to protect the liberty of the people.

Thomas Jefferson gave expression to this political individualism in his speeches and writings. In the Declaration of Independence he proclaimed that liberty along with life and the pursuit of happiness are unalienable rights of each person and that governments are formulated for the purpose of upholding these rights. Jefferson also thought that we must place our trust in the will of the people. He stated in his first inaugural address that "absolute acquiescence in the decisions of the majority" is one of the essential features of government.[1] At the same time, however, he insisted that we should not forget the rights of the minority. He said,

> All, too, will bear in mind this sacred principle, that though the will of the majority is in all cases to prevail, that will, to be rightful, must be reasonable; that the minority possess their equal rights, which equal laws must protect, and to violate would be oppression.[2]

Both economic and political individualism also contained a concept which on the surface appears to be primarily a communal element but in reality turns out to have more of an individualistic influence. This is the concept of a social contract which came especially from two British philosophers, Thomas Hobbes and John Locke. In the seventeenth and eighteenth centuries they claimed that man in his natural state is selfish and greedy and will readily take advantage of others. Consequently, it is in the best interest of each person to enter into a social compact and to establish a political structure. This government regulates the relationships in society and provides security for each individual, but it allows all persons to maximize their own self-interests as long as the accepted guidelines are followed. In fact, the pursuit of self-interest is to be encouraged, for it is this individual quest for private gain that produces the overall good for society.

This final idea soon found a place in American thinking. The emphasis that developed was upon individual initiative and the quest for wealth, and the conviction was that if each person would seek economic advancement, then this would improve the well-being of the whole. As each individual seeks to work harder and to produce more material goods, this will result in the progress of society.

Religious individualism has also been a part of American society since its origin. Our religious thinking has been largely shaped by Protestant Christianity which to a great extent has promoted an individualistic approach to God. It has insisted that in experiencing God a person does not need intermediaries such as the church and the sacraments. Instead, each person relates to God directly and must decide for oneself what kind of relationship this will be. Erich Fromm summarizes this development in the following way:

> In the Catholic Church the relationship of the individual to God had been based on membership in the Church. The Church was the link between him and God, thus on the one hand restricting his individuality, but on the other hand letting him face God as an integral part of a group. Protestantism made the individual face God alone. Faith in Luther's sense was an entirely subjective experience and with Calvin the conviction of salvation also had this same subjective quality.[3]

It should be pointed out that although Luther and Calvin gave very little attention to the contribution of the church to an individual's relationship to God, there have been Protestant groups at various times which have suggested the importance of the guidance and support of others for the individual's salvation process. However, generally speaking, Protestantism has emphasized a kind of religious individualism. For the most part, it has stressed that salvation is predominantly an individual decision, and some Protestant movements have affirmed an approach in which the person is viewed as being completely alone before God. This individualism has been manifested by the numerous revival movements that have occurred in our country over the years. The evangelistic preaching in these movements has typically portrayed each person as having an individual decision to make before God. An example of one of these movements is what has been called The Great Awakening of the 1730s and 1740s. In these meetings preachers such as Jonathan Edwards and George Whitefield called upon the people to repent of their sins, avoid eternal punishment, and be joined with God. These sermons made little or no reference to community ideas such as church assistance, social involvement, and seeking the public good.

Another facet of this religious individualism is what has become known as the Protestant Work Ethic. This was a concept set forth by Calvin and which became a part of the theology of the Puritans. It grew out of the doctrine that man is predestined to be either one of the elect or one of the condemned. Neither society nor anyone else can know about another person's destiny. Only a person's own conscience can provide an answer for this by confronting and interacting with God. But a person who is aware of being one of the elect will feel and act like it. The person will be grateful and will reveal this gratitude by increasing the production of goods. There will be an effort by the individual to work hard for the glory of God, and in return there will be the reward of material success. God rewards those who are among the elect and who work diligently for him.

Thus, religious individualism has been present in the American tradition along with economic and political individualism. In addition, in the eighteenth and nineteenth centuries there were also several influential writers whose ideas promoted various aspects of individualism. One of these was Benjamin Franklin who wrote about the importance of the self-made man. According to Franklin it is possible for an individual to attain virtue and happiness and at the same time live a life which promotes what is best for others. But this can occur only if one's passions and irrationality are restrained by deliberately developing good habits in life. These habits include the practices of self-discipline, frugality, personal initiative, and diligence. Franklin said that "Early to bed and early to rise, makes a man healthy, wealthy, and wise"[4] and that "God helps them that help themselves."[5] Along with this, Franklin warned against laziness and wasting time. He stated that "Laziness travels so slowly that Poverty soon overtakes him"[6] and that "Lost time is never found again."[7]

Furthermore, for Franklin, these individualistic practices also aid one in attaining wealth. Wealth, to him, was a worthy goal, and he sought to give instructions about how to reach it. But it played more of an instrumental role for him than a terminal one. That is, he thought of wealth not so much as something to be sought for its own sake, but more as something that assists one in gaining and maintaining certain other values. He thought that wealth helps to give one a sense of self-respect and provides more time for cultivating the mind. It also increases one's opportunities for benefiting others and making contributions to society.

Horatio Alger was also a proponent of the idea of the self-made man. Alger wrote in the latter half of the nineteenth century when America was becoming industrialized and people were moving from the country to the town or city. Dreams developed and were circulated that one could go to a town or city and make a lot of money. Numerous writers who utilized this theme became popular, but the most well-known and influential was Alger. He wrote about one hundred novels, and the popularity of his works continued on into the early decades of the twentieth century.

Alger's books had a special appeal to young men. The heroes in his writings were often teen-age boys who succeeded in an adult world. They usually would start out poor and end up wealthy, and it was clear from the stories that their achievements were due primarily to their hard work and determination. Undoubtedly, Alger's novels and the desire to go from rags to riches enticed many country boys to leave the farm and seek their fortunes in the city.

Alger's view of self-improvement, therefore, is like Franklin's in that it demands that one be industrious. However, there is also a significant difference in their approaches in that Alger adds the element of luck. In Alger's writings, luck is frequently a contributing factor toward the individual's ability to achieve. In his novel entitled *Ragged Dick*, for example, Dick is a shoeshine boy who rescues a child that has fallen off a ferryboat. The child's father turns out to be a businessman who, out of appreciation, gives Dick a job, providing Dick the opportunity he needs to become wealthy.

Therefore, both Franklin and Alger stressed self-improvement and the idea of the self-made man. Another aspect of individualism was set forth by Ralph Waldo Emerson in the nineteenth century. In his writings and speeches, Emerson called upon Americans to become more independent in their thinking. In his address, "The American Scholar," he insisted that people in this country were overly dependent upon the past and the European tradition and were already suspected of being timid, imitative, and tame. Instead, he said, "We will walk on our own feet; we will work with our own hands; we will speak our own minds."[8] He also argued that scholars in particular have a responsibility to practice self-trust and independent thinking. They must be courageous and speak freely and truthfully from their inward selves.

In his essay entitled "Self-Reliance," Emerson spoke of how society can be a threat to the individual by wanting conformity to what others say. He contended that we must learn to do what we think we should do and not simply what others insist that we do. We must learn to trust in ourselves. He said,

> What I must do is all that concerns me, not what the people think. This rule, equally arduous in actual and in intellectual life, may serve for the whole distinction between greatness and meanness. It is the harder because you will always find those who think they know what is your duty better than you know it. It is easy in the world to live after the world's opinion; it is easy in solitude to live after our own; but the great man is he who in the midst of the crowd, keeps with perfect sweetness the independence of solitude.[9]

Emerson applied this same notion of independent thinking to religion in his "Divinity School Address." He admonished his listeners to quit relying so much upon tradition and to give more attention to God's revelation within them. Preaching, he said, was characterized too much by an adherence to the past and in that sense came out of the memory instead of the soul. It heavily depended upon model personalities and for that reason was not natural and was doomed to mediocrity. He contended that to be genuine and effective, preaching must give expression to the inward beauty of one's own self.

Along with Emerson, Henry David Thoreau was also a writer in the nineteenth century who took a firm stand in support of independent thinking. Thoreau presented his appeal in terms of people needing to decide for themselves the kind of life they will follow. He said, "I would have each one be very careful to find out and pursue his own way, and not his father's or mother's, or his neighbor's instead."[10] However, according to Thoreau, in order to discover one's own way of life, a person must avoid becoming a slave to the conventions of society. Thoreau thought that most people are caught up in simply living in the way that is expected of them by others. This results in their lives being lived in a hurry and in a quest for possessions and comforts. Consequently, they are not only unable to enjoy life, but also they never understand who they really are.

In addition to this theory of independent life, there is also another element of individualism set forth by Thoreau. This is the idea of a period of time in which one becomes detached from society. In 1845 Thoreau built a cabin in the woods on Walden Pond near Concord, Massachusetts, and lived there by himself for two years and two months. During this time he was engaged in reading, writing, communing with nature, and meditating about life. But most of all, he wanted to determine the essentials of life, what we really need in our daily lives as opposed to what we would be better off without. He said that what he discovered was that so much of what we desire and seek is not really necessary. Most people need to simplify their lives and concentrate on that which is truly important. They need to decrease their activities and wants and pay more attention to understanding themselves and appreciating life. Thoreau insisted,

> Simplicity, simplicity, simplicity! I say let your affairs be as two or three, and not a hundred or a thousand; instead of a million count half a dozen, and keep your accounts on your thumbnail. . . . Simplify, simplify. Instead of three meals a day, if it be necessary eat but one; instead of a hundred dishes, five; and reduce other things in proportion.[11]

THE HERITAGE OF COMMUNITY

Hence, over the years, the concept of individualism has become part of American thinking in a variety of ways, but it is also the case that the spirit of community has had a considerable impact upon the American outlook. Of course, a strong contributor to the communal elements in American thought has been the Christian religion. The biblical concepts of the Old Testament covenant and the New Testament church have been especially influential in this regard. The covenant is the idea of the Hebrew people being joined together in an agreement with God. The Hebrews viewed themselves in this covenant as promising to worship God and be loyal to his teachings and in turn the Divine would bless and protect them. When the Hebrews failed in their responsibilities and broke the covenant, then God withdrew his assistance, and they were punished.

The Hebrew concept of the covenant in the Old Testament is presented more in terms of being a collective agreement. The individual's relationship with God is understood more from the perspective of group belonging and the way the group relates to God. In the New Testament, however, the person's relationship to God is viewed more as an individual decision. There is a sense in which the covenant concept continues, but it is more of an agreement which each person makes with God. At the same time, the notion of group belonging and community also continues in the New Testament through the concept of the church. The church consists of those persons who have professed faith in Christ and are joined together with shared beliefs and values. These persons not only worship and learn together but also enjoy each other's fellowship and work together to reach goals. Moreover, each participant of the church is responsible for practicing certain loving qualities both toward others within the church and those not a part of it. Included among those qualities are caring, empathy, compassion, forgiveness, giving, and self-sacrifice.

Therefore, these ideas of the Old Testament covenant and the New Testament church are community concepts in the sense that they include elements such as belonging, cooperation, involvement, and benevolence. These concepts have been expressed in American society over the years through different forms of the Christian religion, but the New England Puritans were an early Christian group that strongly voiced these concepts and also had a significant influence upon later Americans. The Puritans saw themselves as being joined together in a Divine mission. They considered themselves to be like the Hebrews of the Old Testament in that they were also called by God to establish a new society. They thought of themselves as being the new Israel, and America was seen as the promised land. They were specially chosen by God to establish a perfect society in the new world, a visible kingdom of God. This was to be a society of the elect, and one had to give clear evidence of a salvation experience before being fully accepted into the group.

Furthermore, the Puritans viewed their work and responsibilities as a means of assisting the entire community and not simply as a way of benefiting themselves. They saw themselves as involved in a cooperative endeavor to carry out a common purpose. John Winthrop, the first leader of the Massachusetts Bay Colony, clearly set forth the need for this communal attitude in 1630 in his famous sermon on board ship before landing in the new world. In his sermon, he called upon the people to identify closely with each other and to work together as though they were one person. He tells them,

> We must entertain each other in brotherly affection; we must be willing to abridge ourselves of our superfluities, for the supply of others' necessities; we must uphold a familiar commerce together in all meekness, gentleness, patience, and liberality. We must delight in each other, make others' conditions our own, rejoice together, mourn together, labor and suffer together: always having before our eyes our commission and community in the work, our community as members of the same body.[12]

Besides Puritanism, there was another Christian movement that especially emphasized community. This was the social gospel movement which arose in the latter part of the nineteenth century and continued into the early part of the twentieth century. It was a response within the church to the industrial revolution and the corruption of large scale capitalism. Up until this time the church for the most part had concentrated on individual salvation and had ignored social issues. It largely had supported the unaltered acquisition of wealth by big industries and had passively accepted the exploitation of the working class. But persons such as Walter Rauschenbusch and Washington Gladden began to argue that the gospel is concerned with society as well as the individual and that the church has a responsibility to help alleviate social problems. They insisted that each person is part of society and to minister to the individual in the proper manner one must improve society. In their reform activities they particularly addressed the problems of labor. They opposed the children working and advocated labor organizations, increased wages, and better working conditions.

Thus, Puritanism and the social gospel movement represent approaches with communal elements that were direct expressions of the Christian church. However, there were other communal influences in the past that were not as closely related to the church. Although to some extent these may have been affected by Christianity they were also affected by other sources, and sometimes in a significant manner. For example, a communal concept that arose in the eighteenth century was largely derived from Charles Montesquieu, a French political philosopher. This was the idea of republican virtue which had a heavy impact upon the thought of Thomas

Jefferson as well as other early American leaders. According to Montesquieu in a democracy the motivation to uphold the structure of society must come from within in that there must be this inward virtue of loving one's country. This is basically an appreciation of equality of opportunity and frugal practices in society along with a respect for the law. It also implies a willingness to act on behalf of the common good and demands that a person perform certain duties for one's country. There must be the willingness to renounce personal interests and accept responsibilities of service for the whole group. Montesquieu further argued that this virtue is conducive to moral purity within the individual. He claimed that when this virtue is truly present, our attention is given more to the public good and less to our private passions.

An additional part of our community heritage has been certain humanitarian movements and concerns supporting benevolence, social involvement, and the common good. In the eighteenth century Benjamin Franklin was a leading figure in this regard. He gave both his money and personal services for the advancement of libraries, colleges, and hospitals. He also developed various innovative techniques for fund raising including the listing of prospective donors, visitation to seek contributions, and the use of the press for communicating information. These ideas were used by fund-raising organizations on into the nineteenth century and have served as a foundation for the methods used in the twentieth century.

A social reform movement occurred in the late eighteenth and early nineteenth centuries which emphasized that a society does not have the right to achieve its goals at the expense of those who are disadvantaged. It gave attention to such issues as assisting helpless and exploited children, abolishing slavery, increasing the rights of women, and improving the treatment of the mentally ill and handicapped. This movement also included charitable societies which were voluntary groups seeking to aid the poor. They sought to help the poor become self-supporting, if they were unemployed, and made an effort to deal with their problems in a personal way. They visited with the poor and offered them friendly understanding and advice.

In the latter part of the nineteenth century and the early part of the twentieth century there was an increased apppreciation for philanthropy in American society. Multimillionaries such as Andrew Carnegie and John Rockefeller donated large sums of money to improve the quality of life within the country. Contributions were made for scientific research, new programs in colleges, vocational training, and the construction and support of libraries, museums, and recreational facilities. The prevalent rationale for these practices was that a person of great wealth had an obligation to make gifts for the enrichment of society. Carnegie, for instance, insisted that a millionaire should be ashamed to die rich. Rich people, he argued, must use their wealth to provide opportunities for those who are competent and hardworking to advance themselves.

These humanitarian activities, therefore, are another manifestation of the community spirit of the American past. A national leader who particularly portrayed this spirit in the nineteenth century was Abraham Lincoln. He had deep compassion for the people of both the North and the South and wanted to prevent further conflict between them. His concern was to preserve the unity of the two groups and to protect the interest of the nation as a whole. This attitude was set forth in his first inaugural address on March 4, 1861. At that time several Southern states had already seceded from the Union, but nevertheless Lincoln made a passionate appeal for harmony between the North and the South. He sought to assure the South that he did not intend to be the aggressor. He stated that even though it was his duty to execute the nation's laws, he would seek to do it without an invasion or the use of force. He also pleaded with the people of the South to allow time for the problems of the nation to be worked out through a peaceful means. He insisted that intelligence, patriotism, Christianity, and a firm reliance on God were still sufficient to overcome the difficulty. In his conclusion Lincoln reminded the dissatisfied that he still considered them to be friends and that there was a common tie that held all of them together. He stated,

> We are not enemies, but friends. We must not be enemies. Though passion may have strained, it must not break our bonds of affection. The mystic cords of memory, stretching from every battle-field, and patriot grave, to every living heart and hearth-stone, all over this broad land, will yet swell the chorus of the Union, when again touched, as surely they will be, by the better angels of our nature.[13]

INDIVIDUALISM AND COMMUNITY TODAY

Hence, within the American tradition there are certain approaches affirming community along with others that support individualism. These two clusters of values have existed side by side in the past, and each remains very much a part of the American situation. Both of these concepts are expressed in a variety of ways in our society today and no doubt many examples could be mentioned. But the discussion in this chapter will be restricted to some of the most prevalent.

One of the components of individualism in present day society is the idea of making something of oneself. There is still a strong emphasis within our culture upon self-improvement and becoming a person considered worthwhile. Consequently, a person must work hard, be competitive, seek to make more money, and acquire a respectable position in society. For some these goals imply that they diligently pursue a college education and even a graduate degree, and for others it demands that they go to a vocational school and learn a trade. But also there are those for whom this simply means that they must get a job and stay with it. Regardless of the particular path chosen, the idea is that people should make the effort to become more than what they have been.

It is interesting to note that until recently this notion of making something of oneself had an entirely different meaning for women. In fact, in the way that it was defined by such authors as Franklin and Alger, it didn't even apply to women. For these writers, as well as for society in general at that time, the idea was strictly one of the self-made male. Women not only were not expected to have jobs in society, to compete, and to make money, but also were often criticized or laughed at when they became involved in these endeavors. It can be said that there was a sense in which society directed women to make something of themselves, but it was solely through their work in the family that this could be accomplished. They were supposed to perform household duties, raise children, support their husbands, and uphold the family structure. Today the situation is quite different in that many women have joined the world that was previously confined to men. Increasingly in today's society women are defining "improving oneself" and "becoming something" to include making money and having a vocational role.

Another individualistic element in contemporary society is now being applied more extensively to women than in the past. This view usually accompanies the notion of being self-made, but its particular emphasis is upon becoming self-supporting. Although Emerson never discussed his idea of self-reliance in relation to the economic realm, it certainly has been a popular understanding in twentieth century America. Young people in their late teens or at least by their early twenties are expected to begin to break away from their parents and become financially independent. This implies that they get jobs, use their own money, provide for their own needs, and perhaps even have their own place to live.

This concept was not as problematic for young people earlier in this century when high school was usually accepted as the end of the educational venture. In the last several decades with society encouraging education beyond high school, this has become more troublesome. Sometimes parents expect their children to be completely or largely self-supporting and at the same time continue a heavy involvement in college work or vocational training. Also, there are youths who become intent upon gaining financial independence and refuse all forms of parental assistance. When attitudes such as these are held, the results may be detrimental for young people in the sense of causing unnecessary hardships or preventing further education.

Of course, becoming self-supporting can be constructive for the individual when it is properly attained. But so often in our present society it is more beneficial when it is acquired in a gradual manner over a number of years. Difficulties frequently arise when being self-sufficient is interpreted in an all or nothing fashion so that the transition to financial independence is too abrupt. That is, at a certain point in their lives such as at marriage or graduation from high school or college young people may be expected to move suddenly from being nearly totally dependent to being almost entirely self-reliant. This type of approach not only may restrict opportunities and cause unnecessary suffering for young people but also may not provide them adequate time for learning how to manage their financial affairs.

However, it is not merely young people moving into adulthood who are expected to be financially self-supporting in our society. All adults are supposed to practice self-reliance, and those who do not may be frowned upon. This idea is often a contributing cause for the hostile feelings that sometimes exist toward people who rely on our governmental welfare system. Those accepting welfare payments are easily stereotyped as simply being lazy or unwilling to take the initiative to support themselves. Undoubtedly this description is fairly accurate for some welfare recipients, but for most this generality is either untrue or a gross oversimplification. There are many on welfare who are unable to find work and others who are injured, handicapped, physically ill, or mentally ill.

In addition to these economic expressions of individualism, there is also a kind of religious individualism that is practiced in our society today. Its basic characteristic is that a person's religious experiences are for the most part restricted to a direct relationship to God. A person's encounter with the Divine is defined as being one which completely or primarily involves that individual and God. In this approach revelation to an individual through other people, society, or nature is given very little consideration. This kind of indirect communication with God is either entirely excluded from being a part of a person's experience of God or is treated as being secondary in importance.

The other characteristics of religious individualism are to a great extent an outgrowth of this view of Divine revelation. Various events and activities are interpreted and evaluated in accordance with how they are related to the individual's direct experience of God. Social problems are not given priority because they are perceived as being far removed from the individual's religious situation. Also, teaching and education, even when they are obviously religious, do not have the same level of significance as preaching, worship, and prayer because they are not considered to be as closely connected with the individual's encounter with God. Furthermore, acts of fellowship and interaction with others may be thought of as enjoyable and uplifting, but they usually are not regarded as possibly being experiences of God or part of the salvation process.

Moreover, individualism is also manifested today through the individual heroes that appear in movies and television. These heroes are of different types, but one that has had considerable influence throughout this century is the cowboy. He is one who usually either rides alone or has only one companion, but regardless of the odds, he is willing to stand on his own and use his skills to fight against evil and corruption. Another type of hero that has gained prominence more in recent decades is the detective or private investigator. He also usually stands alone or with a single partner and seeks to support what is right and just. He is tough, smart, courageous, and willing to help the unfortunate and unprotected.

It is easy in our society to become captivated by these heroes and not be able to recognize their limitations. Some of them are unreal characters in the sense that they never make any mistakes, don't have any weaknesses, and may not even seem to be subject to temptations. There are also those among them who are too quick to use physical force and are too prone to violence. Furthermore, sometimes they live rather isolated lives and have only casual relationships with others. However, it is true that these heroes sometimes represent a high level of individualism. Many have admirable characteristics and in numerous ways are worthy of being emulated.

Thus, individualism remains active in contemporary American society, but the concept of community also continues to be present today. One way that community occurs is through group participation. There are certain groups in our country that frequently manifest communal qualities and encourage persons toward a community attitude. Of these groups, undoubtedly the family provides the greatest impetus in this direction. Even though the family structure in the United States has been weakened in recent decades by an increasing number of divorces and separations, the family is still the leading communal group in the sense of furnishing people with experiences of this kind. Of course, there are people whose families offer them very little in the way of community experiences, but for a large number of people the fulfillment of their need for feelings of belonging, dependency, and intimacy comes to a great extent from their families.

Other groups also contribute communal qualities to people's lives. For some people religious organizations are a basis for collective experiences in that they give people the opportunity for fellowship and communication with others. Through their teachings they also stress commitment and in some instances involvement in society. Furthermore, there are athletic, musical, political, civic, and professional groups in our society which may be communal. They make possible experiences of companionship and cooperation, and some of them emphasize the common good.

Another communal element today is the continuation of humanitarian interest. There are many fund-raising organizations that have a variety of goals such as helping the sick and unfortunate, financing research for overcoming diseases, and seeking to solve social problems. There are also many examples of large scale philanthropy. Wealthy individuals donate large sums of money not only to fund-raising organizations but also to establish and upgrade hospitals, colleges, and libraries. The idea that the wealthy ought to contribute to the enrichment of society is still popular. This view often results in a certain pattern in the lives of many Americans. In the younger adult years individuals concentrate on career activities and building a fortune with only minor concern for humanitarian efforts. Then in the later years of life when one's career is almost ended and large sums of money have been acquired, attention is given to contributing to the betterment of society.

An additional area of community in contemporary society concerns a certain kind of national interest. There is little doubt that overall the American sense of devotion to country and optimism about the future is not as strong as it was in the eighteenth century or even as it was in the first half of this century. Events such as the Viet Nam war and the Watergate scandal have served to weaken the American spirit. Yet, there still are many people, including especially certain military personnel and some of the governmental employees in Washington, who see themselves as being involved in working for the welfare of the whole country. Also, many others would be willing to offer their services if a national crisis were to arise. These people usually have a deep appreciation for this country and are interested in its well-being. Moreover, even those who reject various policies of the federal government are for the most part not being critical of the country as a whole and are not opposed to the basic principles on which this country was founded. In fact, many of these people are highly concerned about the present circumstances within this country as well as our future direction in international relations.

Public interest still exists in the United States although it is not universal and is not harmonious in terms of a political philosophy. It also may be expressed in different ways and sometimes is even suppressed and hidden. But nevertheless it exists among a significant number of the population.

Furthermore, there exists a communal attitude within this society which views Americans as belonging to a special culture. This attitude differs from the outlook of the Puritans in that some forms of it are not presented in a religious context or thought of in terms of a Divine mission. It also is not as strong a community concept as the Puritan idea in that generally it does not give as much attention to identifying with others and cooperating with them. Additionally, the present viewpoint is not affirmed by as large a percentage of the people as the Puritan concept was and is usually not as intensively held. However, the current understanding is analogous to the Puritan notion in that it does think of Americans as being unique. Some see this more in terms of our personal freedom and democratic government, whereas others emphasize our capitalistic system of free enterprise. There are also still those who are closely aligned with the Puritans because they consider us to be favored by God and chosen by him to carry out special tasks. Even though there may be several different perspectives that are set forth, a common trait is shared by each of these views. All of them regard Americans as being a distinctive group.

There is a final element of community in contemporary American society which should be mentioned. This is one which parallels the notion of the individual hero and is particularly portrayed through television. Many of the dramatic serials and situation comedies that are popular on television today center around family circumstances. These shows often glamorize the material and strongly emphasize the value of making money. They also may be preoccupied with sexuality and illicit love affairs. At the same time there is a kind of communal spirit that usually is present in the midst of all this. The family context allows for feelings of belonging and togetherness, and at times there are expressions of kindness, empathy, and cooperation among family members. However, it is interesting to note that it is not uncommon for other aspects of community to be ignored or even rejected by these shows. Those who are outside the family, for instance, may be treated with indifference, ridicule, or disdain, and also there is little concern with helping to solve social problems or seeking the common good.

THE TENSION BETWEEN INDIVIDUALISM AND COMMUNITY

Individualism and community not only have an extensive heritage in American society but also play a vital part in the culture today. However, these are not simply two different outlooks present within American thought. That is, these approaches cannot be easily separated from one another and decided upon individually. Instead, they interact with each other and contain opposing qualities. This gives rise to a certain amount of tension between them in the sense that they frequently create conflicts for Americans as they make decisions and develop a style of life. This tension between these concepts was recognized by an early French visitor to the

United States by the name of Alexis de Toqueville. He came to America in 1831 in order to assess the merits of this new society and especially its democratic structure. During his visit he noted the significant role that individualism plays in American thinking and how to some extent it is counterbalanced by certain tendencies toward community.

Tocqueville viewed individualism as a perspective which grows out of the democratic system in American society and as being the principal charac- teristic of the philosophical method common to Americans. He described it as the disposition to separate oneself from the mass of one's fellow human beings and to appeal only to the solitary effort of one's own understanding. He said there is a sharp distinction between this outlook and that which is prevalent in the aristocratic societies of Europe. In aristocracies people typically think in terms of having duties toward their ancestors and descen- dents, and they usually derive many of their ideas from their own class. In a democratic society with its individualism, this is not the case. Americans tend to think in terms of owing nothing to anyone else and of expecting nothing in return. Also, since there is no class structure in the United States for the most part, they do not rely on the views of others or think of others as being superior to them. Americans think of themselves more as standing alone, and they are apt to imagine that their whole destiny is in their own hands.

According to Tocqueville, this individualistic element within a democ- racy has the potential for destruction. It can easily lead to extreme selfish- ness and alienation from others. Citizens may become absorbed in them- selves or have their interests confined to those who are in proximity to themselves. At the same time, it may result in there being little or no concern for the welfare of society as a whole so that there is a lack of public involvement. Toqueville said that democracy with its individualism does not just make

> every man forget his ancestors, but it hides his descendents and separates his contemporaries from him; it throws him back forever upon himself alone and threatens in the end to confine him entirely within the solitude of his own heart.[14]

Tocqueville, therefore, thought that if individualism were allowed to operate within the American spirit without any restrictions, it would even- tually lead to widespread selfishness and isolation. He also was aware that there were certain countervailing forces within American society which tend to limit the effects of individualism. These forces serve to encourage the American citizen away from a narrow type of individualism and toward a community outlook. One of these grows out of the nature of the democratic system in that freedom and self-government demand that some of the citizens seek public office and attend to public affairs. Additionally, political life in the United States is infused into each portion of the country. This multiplies the opportunities for acting for the benefit of the community and helps people feel their mutual dependence. Furthermore, in a democracy the work of society must be carried out by the citizens themselves, and they quickly realize that they need each other to get things accomplished. They must work together to pursue their common desires and goals. Consequently, there are many associations in American society including those for political purposes and others for commercial, moral, religious, or social reasons. Finally, community is encouraged in American culture by what Tocqueville referred to as the principle of self-interest rightly understood. Americans are able to combine their own advantage with that of their fellow citizens. It is insisted that because sacrifices for others are of benefit to oneself, it is in the interest of every person to be virtuous. An enlightened regard for oneself constantly prompts one to assist others and to be willing to sacrifice for the welfare of the state.

Thus, at an early period in American history Tocqueville recognized not only that the different views of individualism and community were operative in American society but also that to some degree they were pulling people in different directions. This tension between these concepts was present in the past, and it continues today as Americans seek to make value choices. In order to gain a more specific understanding of the nature of this tension, an effort will be made to analyze it in terms of certain basic value conflicts which grow out of individualism and community. These include the contrasting ideas of achievement and benevolence, private interests and the public good, detachment and involvement, and independence and dependence.

NOTES

1. Thomas Jefferson, "First Inaugural Address," *The Complete Jefferson*, ed. Saul Padover (New York: Duell, Sloan and Pearce, Inc., 1943) 386.
2. Ibid., 384.
3. Erich Fromm, *Escape from Freedom* (New York: Holt, Rinehart and Winston, 1941) 108.
4. Benjamin Franklin, *Poor Richard's Almanack* (Mount Vernon, New York: Peter Pauper Press, n.d.) 48.
5. Ibid., 57.
6. Ibid., 73.
7. Ibid., 43.
8. Ralph Waldo Emerson, *Nature, Addresses, and Lectures* (Boston: Houghton, Mifflin and Company, 1876) 115.
9. Ralph Waldo Emerson, *Essays: First Series* (New York: American Publishers Corporation, n.d.) 50.

10. Henry David Thoreau, *Walden* (Boston: Houghton Mifflin Company, 1893) 79.

11. Ibid., 101–102

12. John Winthrop, "A Model of Christian Charity," *The American Puritans*, ed. Perry Miller (Garden City: Doubleday and Company, 1956) 83.

13. Abraham Lincoln, "First Inaugural Address," *Abraham Lincoln: His Speeches and Writings*, ed. Roy Basler (Cleveland: The World Publishing Company, 1946) 588.

14. Alexis de Tocqueville, *Democracy in America* (New York: Alfred A. Knopf, 1945) 2:99.

DISCUSSION QUESTIONS

1. Do you agree with the idea that the good of society as a whole is produced by each individual seeking personal gain? To what extent, if any, is this idea still a part of American thinking?

2. Do you think your own religious background has placed too much emphasis on the individual being alone before God? Has it given sufficient attention to an individual's need for group belonging and the acceptance of others?

3. What is your evaluation of the Protestant Work Ethic? Do you think God rewards people in a material way when they work hard for him?

4. Do you agree with Franklin's view of material wealth? Do you think this wealth has instrumental value? Does it have terminal value?

5. Do you think God reveals himself through the inward self as Emerson insisted? If so, what are some ways that this might occur?

6. How important is Thoreau's idea of simplifying our lives? Should we seek to do this today? If so, what would be some ways of doing this?

7. Do you think that the United States is in some way special? If so, in what sense? Do you think God is especially on the side of Americans in international relations and world conflicts?

8. Do you think the gospel has a social dimension? Does the church have a responsibility to get involved in problems in society such as business and politics?

9. How strong in your judgment is the notion of republican virtue in our society today? Are you able to name any popular ideas or activities which tend to interfere with its acceptance?

10. Do you agree with Carnegie's contention that a millionaire should be ashamed to die rich?

11. If the parents of a young married couple are financially capable, do you think they should give the couple financial assistance when it is needed?

12. What factors would you say contribute to the animosity toward welfare recipients in our society?

13. Give some examples of individual heroes from movies or television who you think are worthy of being emulated. Are there some that you would say definitely should not be emulated? Why?

14. What does it mean to you to be patriotic and love your country? Is it patriotic to be openly critical of the policies of the federal government?

15. What specific values are often promoted today by television shows which are centered around a family situation? Are these constructive in nature?

SUGGESTIONS FOR FURTHER READING

Basler, Roy, ed. *Abraham Lincoln: His Speeches and Writings.* Cleveland: The World Publishing Company, 1946.

Bellah, Robert. *The Broken Covenant.* New York: The Seabury Press, 1975.

Bellah, Robert; Madsen, Richard; Sullivan, William; Swidler, Ann; and Tipton, Steven. *Habits of the Heart.* New York: Harper and Row, 1985.

Emerson, Ralph Waldo. *Essays: First Series.* New York: American Publishers Corporation, n.d.

—————. *Nature, Addresses, and Lectures.* Boston: Houghton, Mifflin and Company, 1876.

Franklin, Benjamin. *The Autobiography of Benjamin Franklin.* New York: Washington Square Press, 1955.

—————. *Poor Richard's Alamanack.* Mount Vernon, New York: Peter Pauper Press, n.d.

Fromm, Erich. *Escape from Freedom.* New York: Holt, Rinehart and Winston, 1941.

Miller, Perry, ed. *The American Puritans.* Garden City: Doubleday and Company, 1956.

Padover, Saul, ed. *The Complete Jefferson.* New York: Duell, Sloan and Pearce, Inc., 1943.

Thoreau, Henry David. *Walden.* Boston: Houghton Mifflin Company, 1893.

Tocqueville, Alexis de. *Democracy in America.* New York: Alfred A. Knopf, 1945.

Whittemore, Robert. *Makers of the American Mind.* New York: William Morrow and Company, 1964.

CHAPTER 2
ACHIEVEMENT AND BENEVOLENCE

Two sets of values within individualism and community that have sometimes resulted in conflicts in decision making are indicated by the ideas of achievement and benevolence. For Americans achievement has usually meant that we should be ambitious, aggressive, competitive, striving, and hard working in order to accomplish our goals in life. In general this concept simply means to reach the established goals. One of the typical goals highly regarded in American society is material gain in that the individual thinks in terms of making more money or having more material possessions. Another is the attainment of some form of appreciation or recognition from others such as acquiring a high social status or becoming popular or famous.

Regardless of the specific way that achievement is understood by the individual, the emphasis of this group of values has usually been upon seeking to gain something for oneself. These values may be viewed by the individual in conjunction with an effort to serve God, to contribute to society, or to benefit the lives of others. Certainly this is a possibility, and no doubt there have been Americans who have taken this approach. But even though these values may be viewed in this light, this has not been the immediate and primary emphasis ascribed to them in our culture. These values have traditionally been given a predominantly individual orientation in which the chief concern is for some type of accomplishment for the particular person.

There is an additional set of values in our society which sometimes enters into conflict with achievement. It stresses qualities such as being caring, compassionate, empathetic, giving, and self-sacrificing, but the fundamental belief is that of benevolence or an attitude of consideration and goodwill toward others. Therefore, in contrast to achievement, this group of values is primarily directed toward the welfare of others. This is not to say that these values are never used as a basis for individual achievement. No doubt it is possible to regard these values as merely a means of reaching personal gain. One, for instance, may express concern for someone else or carry out a benevolent act for another as essentially an effort to improve one's own chance of advancement. However, treatment of these values as simply instruments for advancement is not the way they usually have been presented in our society. In fact, our religious traditions generally have looked with disfavor upon this approach and instead have emphasized that the good of others is a worthy goal in itself and that benevolence should be regarded as superior to personal gain.

Thus, there has been a contrast of emphasis within American society between these two groups of values. The collection of values revolving around achievement has given more attention to individual gain, whereas those values centered in benevolence have been directed more toward the welfare of others. This chapter examines this contrast in values in American society. It indicates the manner in which these values have been expressed through the American idea of success and discusses a variety of decisions, both for the individual and within the vocations, which involve these concepts. This chapter also explores the relationship between achievement and benevolence and recommends an approach for understanding this relationship.

THE AMERICAN UNDERSTANDING OF SUCCESS

One way that the contrast between achievement and benevolence has been expressed within American society is through our understanding of success. There are two broad views of success in our society which correspond closely with the sets of values that are represented by achievement and benevolence. These two concepts, which Richard Huber refers to as the cultural and the personal, have existed in our society since its origin and are still active and influential today. Cultural success has been the most prevalent concept of success and is what most Americans think of when the term "success" is mentioned. Although this type of success refers especially to making money and acquiring material possessions, it may also include obtaining power, prestige, and fame. Consequently, the two basic elements of this notion are material wealth and status. But success in this sense is not simply a matter of possessing one or both of these, for the idea of ascent plays an important part in this concept. Cultural success means attaining riches or achieving fame. It is necessary for a person to exceed the past; one must go beyond where one has been.

One measure of cultural ascent has been to do better than one's father by holding a job with higher pay or prestige. For example, a man who is a bank clerk would have a better chance at being thought of as a success if his father had been a janitor rather than a corporation president. By this standard it is easier for an individual to become a success if that person's father has been considered unsuccessful. Another criterion of ascent is the degree to which the individual's working situation has improved since its beginning. A person may have substantially a better job or make more money than at an earlier time and so be considered a cultural success.[1]

Cultural success has also included a distinction between business success and nonbusiness success. For most Americans cultural success has the meaning of business success which refers primarily to making a profit and increasing one's material wealth. But at the same time it does not exclude the element of status in that it demands that money be translated into prestige. That is, business success requires the use of material gain to improve one's social standing. Economic achievement must be converted into social achievement such as, for example, by buying a house in a more prestigious neighborhood.[2]

Even though our society thinks of cultural success more in terms of business success, it has also made room for another kind of cultural success that is not directed toward making a profit. This type of cultural success is applied to jobs such as teaching and church related vocations which carry with them a ceiling on the amount of money that can be made. Consequently, nonbusiness success is defined not by the money that is acquired but by the rank that is achieved. Rank is determined to a certain degree by the public prominence afforded the institution where one works. For instance, a minister in charge of a large well-established church is viewed quite differently from one who heads a small church with little influence. Similarly, a judge on the state supreme court is thought of differently from a local magistrate. Another factor that plays a part in the rank of the nonbusiness individual is the esteem and praise received from the person's institution and profession. Recognition would consist of earning a higher position in the organization or receiving awards and prizes. This factor is sometimes called institutional or professional success because it depends entirely upon the evaluation given by the members of one's institution or profession and not upon that given by the general public.[3]

Cultural success, therefore, includes both business and nonbusiness success. In addition to a cultural understanding of success, another concept that has been operative in American society is called personal success. Even though this notion has not been a familiar use of the term "success" in our society, it does denote an inward perspective on success that Americans have often held. Americans have often thought that success really means being happy and satisfied with life which implies having friends and a good family life. In order for this to occur, a person must be considerate of others and be willing to make sacrifices for the well-being of others. Thus, personal success demands that a person carry out loving acts for others and be more concerned with giving than getting.[4] As Huber says,

True success is within ourselves—in peace of mind or happiness. When it is outside ourselves, it flows from self-giving rather than self-seeking. It is measured by a happy family life or service to others. It flows out of what we are taught is our better selves. It is marked not by what assets we have accumulated in our estate but what good deeds we have sent before.[5]

The research of Daniel Yankelovich indicates that there has been a recent turn in American society toward the personal notion of success. On the basis of his national surveys and interviews, he insists that there has been a growing emphasis on the inward self in the 1970s and 1980s. Although it is still a minority movement, he claims there are more people than in the past who are especially intent upon acquiring self-fulfillment. In order to gain this fulfillment, they want more freedom and more opportunity to express themselves and exercise their creative feelings. This has resulted in extremely difficult decisions for some individuals such as whether to remain within a restrictive or unsatisfying marriage and whether to keep a lucrative and prestigious job even though it may be boring, stressful, or simply unrewarding. Yankelovich says that there is an increasing number of people who are making choices of this nature in a manner which runs counter to traditional social values. They are sacrificing old values such as a high paying job, the approval of others, and a continuing marriage in favor of new values such as fulfillment, freedom, and creativity.[6]

To some extent emphasis on self-fulfillment is like the personal success that Huber describes in that it gives attention to the desire for inward happiness. However, there is also a dissimilarity because the search for inner satisfaction has not always carried with it a benevolent attitude. Sometimes it has merely been a duty-to-self type of ethic. The individuals have at times sought personal fulfillment through an act such as quitting a job without giving proper consideration to the welfare of others.[7]

Furthermore, it is interesting to note that this movement does not represent a rejection of cultural success. Yankelovich says that the campus revolts of the 1960s to a great extent gave rise to the self-fulfillment emphasis, but nonetheless these two movements are not identical. The revolts emphasized a simple life-style and a renunciation of the material. Those seeking fulfillment may be willing at times to give up prestige or money as a way to attain freedom or to express themselves, but this does not imply an overall rejection of material goods and comfort. It is typical of those within the new movement to want both inward satisfaction and material possessions.[8]

Thus, both personal success and cultural success continue to be present, which points to a paradox of values in the American understanding. On the one hand, Americans individually have often thought and felt within themselves that success must be defined in a nonmaterialistic way, that it must be defined in terms of inner contentment, healthy relationships with others, and benevolent acts. On the other hand, society as a whole has strongly promoted a materialistic emphasis and the idea that success must be measured in this manner. Consequently, there has been a great deal of ambivalence on the part of Americans in their approach to success. There is a sense in which a large number of Americans don't really approve of cultural success, but there is also a sense in which so many of these same Americans want to achieve it and are constantly striving for it.[9]

CONFLICTS FOR THE INDIVIDUAL

This long-standing paradox in the American idea of success contributes to the difficulty that Americans frequently have in choosing between the values surrounding achievement and benevolence. There are areas both for the individual and in the institutions of society in which decisions involve conflicts between these values. Sometimes these decisions require that achievement or benevolence must be chosen at the exclusion of the other, but more often they are a matter of determining which one will be given priority and what form the priority will take. In regard to individual decisions involving this conflict, there are numerous examples that could be discussed, but three in particular are often troublesome and at the same time influential and worthy of consideration. One of these is the choice of a vocation. In seeking to make a vocational decision, young people in their late teens and early twenties usually receive a variety of advice from family, friends, the church, and society. One person may tell them that they ought to choose an occupation that will make it possible for them to make a lot of money, and another may say that a prestigious profession such as medicine or law is what they should select. Someone else may instruct them to choose something that they are interested in and which will be meaningful, while a person with a religious perspective may stress that they should decide upon a vocation which is within the will of God and which will be a service to God and humanity.

Fundamental to choosing a vocation is a decision about the criteria for that choice or, in other words, the values to be used in selecting a vocation. An initial decision must be made about the importance to one's work of such things as money, material possessions, status, fulfillment, assisting other people, and serving God. Which value or values will be given priority in the choice of a vocation? Of course, this decision concerning criteria is simultaneously a decision about achievement and benevolence. To what extent, if any, will one's own personal advancement be considered in the selection of a vocation and to what degree, if at all, will the consideration of others be a factor?

Unfortunately certain vocations in American society have been stereotyped as vocations of achievement and others as vocations of benevolence.
Classic examples would be the image of a job in business as a means of
gaining wealth and the notion of work in a religious institution as being
devoted to God and the care of people. In reality any job can be thought of
predominantly in terms of either achievement or benevolence or with
approximately equal emphasis on each of these values. Certainly it is
possible for individuals in any position in the business world, whether self-
employed, working for another, or a member of a large corporation, to
think of their work as benefiting others. Persons in business with this
outlook may also be seeking to structure their work and implement their
activities in a manner which will continually improve upon their ability to
assist others. No doubt this approach, when given heavy attention, may be
difficult to maintain because of social and institutional pressures to do
otherwise. Even if this value is hidden or suppressed in the life of the
individual, it may still remain significant as an ideal; consequently, it may
reemerge and be utilized when the circumstances are appropriate.

Moreover, it is possible for a person to give a large degree of consideration to the value of achievement in approaching a church-related vocation.
In some instances this may take the form of seeking material gain, but
perhaps a stronger possibility in this regard is the pursuit of status or
popularity. When this is the case, such occurrences as a position in a large
church, a building program, an increase in church membership, and the
praise of others are interpreted to a great extent as symbols of personal
achievement.

Another area of individual decisions in which the conflict between
achievement and benevolence arises concerns certain competitive activities
in American life. Being competitive is a strong value in our society and one
which Americans begin to learn at an early age. Americans are not the only
ones who emphasize competition, for other cultures also point to the need
to be competitive and seek to encourage their children and young people in
this direction. However, as Philip Slayter points out, our society seems to lie
near an extreme in this regard. We seem to give greater attention and
encouragement to competitive practices than do most societies.[10]

The American idea of being competitive is closely aligned with achievement in that it is required for a person to achieve. To be competitive means
to try hard and to do one's best in an effort to excel and to win. This concept
is usually defined more in terms of one's relationships with others. That is,
to be involved in competing often has more of the meaning of competing
with others than competing with oneself. In order to reach the goal of
winning or excelling, the person thinks primarily of overcoming other
people instead of improving one's self. It is not so important that there has

been progress by the individual, but rather that the person has done better than others. In addition, an extreme emphasis in competition upon overcoming others can easily lead to thoughts and actions which definitely run counter to benevolence. The person may begin to wish for others to fail or experience misfortune and even at times may be willing to intervene and harm others in some way.

Furthermore, many people in American society do not compete well in many phases of life or for various reasons may simply refuse to compete at all. Because of the strong competitive emphasis in our society, these persons even in childhood are often labeled as failures and looked upon as being lazy or just inept. Sometimes this is an accurate evaluation in that they may be rather lethargic or lack the skill required to excel in competitive activities. But often it is more a matter of these people not having the temperament necessary to be competitive. They may be shy and unwilling to engage aggressively in competitive interaction, or they may be rather tender minded and not want to cause another to lose or be disappointed.

American society, therefore, highly values the development of a competitive attitude, and this frequently contributes to the difficulty of many people in decisions involving achievement and benevolence. A person may affirm the significance of being competitive and excelling but at the same time have certain benevolent feelings toward others and their circumstances. Some aspects of life in which this conflict is especially apparent are school, the work place, sports events, and the home. At school the individual is encouraged by teachers and family members to work hard and make good grades. Some students may be slow to understand, and sometimes other students must decide whether to take time to give assistance. In the work place there is competition between individuals for promotions and better jobs, and decisions have to be made about the degree to which instruction and aid will be offered to fellow workers. Sports events include competition not only with other teams but also with persons on one's own team. Seeking to attain a position on a team carries with it decisions about how far one should go in helping another. At times there may also be competition in the home between brothers and sisters, between parents, and even between parents and children, and these competitive efforts may be directed toward different goals such as the attention of others, the respect of others, the improvement of the family, or simply the desire to feel superior. These relationships give rise to circumstances in which decisions must be made about the extent one should go in being considerate and sacrificing for other family members.

Another area of conflict between achievement and benevolence concerns the way that money is used. A large number of Americans have a financial income that exceeds what is required for them to meet the basic necessities of life, and decisions must be made about the way this additional money will be spent. On the one hand, it may be used to buy extra food, clothing, and living accommodations for oneself and one's family as well as to purchase certain luxuries, conveniences, and enjoyable experiences in life. On the other hand, it may be used to assist others such as through gifts to deserving individuals, constructive social causes, or religious organizations. Therefore, achievement in this sense is spending this money for the purpose of benefiting oneself or one's family, whereas benevolence is using the money in an effort to carry out a compassionate act for another.

Certainly at times it is possible to do both through a single action such as buying a business which increases personal wealth and at the same time assists the community by creating more jobs. However, many choices concerning money force a decision about whether they will be oriented more toward achievement or benevolence. For instance, many people must decide if they will contribute to charities and to religious groups. Frequently in our society people have enough income beyond necessities to spend on personal achievement and benevolence. The question then becomes just how much will be designated to each. Decisions must be made about how far one will go in efforts of achievement and deeds of benevolence and in what way these will be carried out.

In making these decisions it is beneficial to recognize, as Erich Fromm says, that our society places a strong emphasis upon having as a fundamental way of existing. Our society is especially devoted to making money and gaining possessions; consequently, it is often difficult for us to think in terms of giving, sharing, and sacrificing. As Fromm states,

> . . . we live in a society that rests on private property, profit, and power as the pillars of its existence. To acquire, to own, and to make a profit are the sacred and unalienable rights of the individual in the industrial society.[11]

It is even possible to become preoccupied with having and to think that it is the only acceptable way of life. In this case having is something that an individual depends upon for self-identity and is an outlook that seeks to make everything subject to one's own power. Of course, having can take many forms in that there are different ways of having including eating, buying goods, accumulating money, owning land, watching television, and traveling. It may also be expressed in terms of possessing people such as a spouse, a child, a friend, or an employee.[12]

Furthermore, in making decisions concerning the use of money it is necessary to realize, as Peter Singer points out, that our society tends to have a rather limited understanding of duty and charity. A duty is a responsibility which an individual is obligated to carry out; failure to do so is considered wrong. For example, if one agrees to do a certain job and accepts pay for it, it usually is one's duty to perform it, and it is wrong not to. In contrast, an act of charity is a good deed that goes beyond the requirements of one's duty. This type of act is regarded as good, but it is not considered wrong if it is not done. In our society, for instance, donating blood to a hospital or blood center is often treated as a charitable act. It is a worthy act, but it is not thought of as wrong if one does not donate.[13]

In our society, as Singer says, the concept of one's duty is defined too narrowly and the concept of charity is given too broad a meaning.[14] Too many acts are being labeled as charitable and not enough is being expected from individuals in the performance of duty. In other words, there are acts that society tends to regard as charitable which really ought to be thought of as duties. In terms of decisions about spending money, this means that individuals have obligations toward certain benevolent uses of money that are generally being overlooked. That is, there are individual duties in the use of money that are not easily recognized in American society because our social traditions, norms, and values treat them as charitable acts instead of duties. For example, occasions exist for many individuals when they have an obligation to provide a gift or a loan of money to a friend or relative. Another example is the duty that a large number of Americans have to contribute money to deal with poverty and social problems both within this country and in other countries. Although our society usually considers these instances to be acts of charity, in reality for many Americans they should be thought of as duties.

Therefore, in American society it is difficult in decisions about the use of money to give benevolence its due consideration. Various social influences and pressures tend to encourage the individual toward decisions that favor achievement and neglect benevolence. This means that a considerable strength of character is required in these decisions before an individual is able to give proper attention to benevolence. Virtues such as courage, determination, and the willingness to be different are often necessary for this to occur.

CONFLICTS IN THE VOCATIONS

Hence, individuals are confronted by a variety of decisions which involve conflicts between achievement and benevolence. But conflicts between these values occur not only as people make decisions for their personal lives but also as they seek to carry out their vocational responsibilities. Different kinds of achievement perspectives may be adopted by workers as they function within the institutions of society, and some of these outlooks conflict with benevolence. One of these conflicts in the vocations concerns the treatment of employees in business organizations. A prominent form of achievement within organizations demands that maximum efficiency and output be sought from a worker whenever possible, whereas a benevolent approach is more willing to give particular considerations because of the circumstances. There are times, for example, when an employee is not feeling well or perhaps has personal problems, and the question is whether pressure should be put on the worker to maintain the usual level of production or whether allowances should be made because of the difficulty. There is also the situation of the older employee nearing retirement who is unable or unwilling to work at the same level as in the past. In this case there may be the same question of whether pressure should be applied on the person to work harder, but another question that sometimes arises in this situation involves the issue of forced retirement. This is the question of whether some effort should be made to encourage or coerce the employee to retire in order to protect the company or whether consideration should be given to a worker because of age and past contributions to the business. Of course, in some instances, such as when the older worker has an illness, the compassionate act toward the individual worker may be to force retirement.

These questions are complicated because benevolence in these cases can not be defined simply in terms of the worker who is directly affected. A productive business has benefits for each of its employees as well as for the rest of society. It provides economic security to its workers along with goods and/or services to the community. Very often one individual weakness within a business will not jeopardize the welfare of the other workers or the contribution that is being made to society. But circumstances can arise which may be detrimental. For instance, in a small unstable business just one irresponsible or incompetent worker could have serious repercussions for the welfare of the whole. Consequently, in questions regarding the treatment of employees in business, benevolence does not merely give attention to the particular worker that is immediately involved. It also must consider the well-being of the other workers and even what is best for all of society.

An area in religious institutions that may include conflicts between achievement and benevolence concerns the teaching and preaching of church leaders and the ideas that are introduced to the people. Sometimes church leaders consider being liked and approved by the congregation as an important part of their own sense of achievement, and their popularity may be hindered if views are set forth which are controversial or not favored by the majority. Thus, an emphasis on personal advancement in this sense often results in the suppression of certain beliefs and values in order to insure the acceptance of the people. In contrast, benevolence demands that at times new and possibly unpopular notions be enunciated both for the sake of truth and for the improvement of the people. Of course, benevolence takes into consideration that individuals have a variety of levels of understanding and at the same time seeks to stimulate personal growth at a pace that is realistic and wholesome. It also seeks to avoid introducing concepts just for the sake of appearing knowledgeable or distinctive. Nevertheless, when necessary, benevolence is willing to discuss controversial issues and to publicly affirm a position that may not be accepted by the majority.

It is possible to claim that the suppression of ideas actually represents the stance of benevolence. That is, it is sometimes thought that benevolence in this regard would seek to protect individuals from possible false viewpoints and from the pain of struggling with new ideas. Also, it may further be argued that the introduction of controversial concepts may result in turmoil or dissension within the congregation and is therefore more of a negative factor than a positive one. In response to this attitude toward benevolence it must first be pointed out that such an approach is not always genuine and may merely represent a rationalization by the individual in order to continue being accepted by the majority. The view may be affirmed not because it is thought to be true but because it enables the person to avoid saying something controversial or unpopular. However, to those who authentically accept this approach it should be made clear that it does not represent the full meaning of benevolence. It may appear in the immediate sense that compassion demands the exclusion of unpopular ideas and discourages disagreements within the group, but to do so is not really compassionate. Benevolence requires that people confront new perspectives and that they learn to examine them and decide for themselves what they believe accurate. In this way people are able to develop their own understandings and gain personal confidence in their truth. This process is not always easy because of the uncertainty and anxiety that it often involves; nevertheless, it is necessary to foster personal growth and maturity in the individual.

In addition, benevolence deems it important that people have an environment that allows them to disagree with each other. Of course, efforts should be made to promote disagreements that are healthy so that they maintain respect for other people and their rights to their own outlooks on life. It is at this point that leaders can offer a valuable form of assistance by structuring discussions and encouraging positive interaction. When this kind of environment is properly established, it offers excellent opportunities for the development of the individual. People are able to be open with their new ideas and avoid the guilt that might otherwise be present from keeping them private, and they are also able to grow through an honest interchange with the views of others.

An issue in the area of health care containing a conflict between achievement and benevolence involves decisions about the number of patients and the fees that are charged. One type of achievement orientation on the part of health care workers such as medical doctors and dentists is interested in treating a large number of patients each day. It may also insist upon charging as high a fee as possible for the services rendered and refuse to reduce these charges regardless of the circumstances. In contrast, benevolence is more concerned with the quality of treatment given to each patient than with trying to see a quantity of patients. It is willing to take the time necessary for careful and comprehensive attention to the circumstances of patients and to be able to communicate clearly with them. Benevolence also seeks to set fair and reasonable fees for various treatments and is willing to reduce these charges and even at times cancel them completely because of the financial limitations of certain patients.

Health care workers often have to treat many patients in a day. Also, there may be a scarcity of medical personnel in a given area, or there may be workers who are sick or on vacation. In this case benevolence may require that less attention be given to each patient in order to meet the needs of a large number. However, benevolence seeks to avoid making this a consistent practice, and even when it is necessary, benevolence insists upon maintaining as high a quality of health care as possible.

Furthermore, in setting fees for patients benevolence considers the welfare of health care personnel and also the need to uphold the level of the working environment. Money must be available to pay adequate salaries and to provide funds for the needed facilities and equipment. At the same time benevolence is not willing to inflate fees simply because it is permissible by society and the profession or because it is necessary to support an exorbitant life-style. Benevolence always demonstrates a sense of concern for the whole person including the financial status of the patient.

Another conflict between achievement and benevolence in the professions occurs in education in decisions concerning relationships with students. Teachers have to make decisions in their work about the structure of classes and the treatment of students. Sometimes an achievement perspective on the part of teachers takes the form of being preoccupied with establishing and maintaining one's own academic reputation. When this motivation is present, the teacher is especially concerned with making an impressive appearance and being thought of as highly knowledgeable and skillful by students and others. Consequently, attention is given to organizing and conducting the class in a manner that is conducive to this effect. Also, students usually are not permitted to challenge the views of the teacher, and there may be a severely critical approach toward students who express different outlooks from the teacher. The teacher frequently doesn't allow any type of class discussion which involves debate and close interaction and may even seek to avoid discussions with students altogether. When there is a class discussion, an effort is often made to direct the focus toward those areas with which the teacher is most familiar.

On the other hand, benevolence on the part of the teacher gives special attention to the needs of students. Decisions about methods of teaching, issues to be studied, and ways of relating are made on the basis of what will best contribute to the abilities, the understanding, and the development of students. Benevolence may decide, for example, that students ought to study certain material or be exposed to it in a lecture even though it may at first be unknown to the teacher or a difficult topic to teach. Furthermore, a benevolent emphasis seeks to enter into an open, give-and-take discussion with students and tries to encourage honest responses regardless of their nature. Students are expected to examine carefully all of the views, even those of the teacher, in order to decide for themselves what is correct.

These varying approaches in education are usually clearly revealed in the confrontation with a hostile and bitter student. Teachers with an achievement orientation of the type previously indicated usually consider those students who are resentful and extremely critical as being threats to their reputation. As a result, it is common for these students to be treated in a rather condescending and spiteful fashion to convince them of their inferior position. Their statements and questions may be largely ignored or cut short, or they may be sharply rebuked or ridiculed.

However, a benevolent teacher is sensitive to the overall welfare of students and, therefore, responds to this kind of attitude in a different manner. In some cases this teacher may find it necessary to talk to these students privately outside of class to establish closer relationships and at the same time assist them in constructively confronting their own attitudes and views. In many situations the teacher may merely allow these students to express their ideas in class and encourage them to think about why they accept them. This attitude acknowledges the value of these students and their right to have their own views, but it also may aid them in more fully recognizing their animosity toward the teacher and the emotional nature of their position. Moreover, even though benevolence seeks to treat students of this type compassionately and not to unnecessarily embarrass them, this approach must be firm and at times may need to show students their weaknesses directly. This may be required in order to assist them in gaining not only knowledge and thinking skills but also respect and self-control.

The Relationship Between Achievement and Benevolence

Thus, there are both decisions for the individual and decisions within the various professions which involve conflicts between achievement and benevolence. Every one of these decisions has a specific and peculiar nature in that each includes particular circumstances and needs which must be taken into consideration. However, it is still beneficial to adopt an overall approach in making these decisions. That is, some assistance can be offered for dealing with choices through the development of a general philosophy of the relationship between achievement and benevolence. But how should this relationship be understood? Should both of these notions be affirmed? Are these concepts to be perceived as being mutually exclusive, or should they be viewed as reconcilable?

In order to answer these questions, it is first necessary to examine these ideas more closely. It is certainly possible to approach achievement as simply being gain for oneself with little regard for others. Indeed, in our culture it is easy to think of achievement in this manner because of the strong social emphasis in this direction. Means of communication and entertainment including advertising, novels, television, and movies often represent personal advancement as a goal an individual ought to pursue for its own sake. Values such as money, status, and fame are frequently presented in terms of their immediate rewards for the individual so that primary focus is given to their worth as ends in themselves. However, achievement does not have to be defined as personal gain that is completely or primarily for one's own benefit. It can be viewed a being to some extent a means of assisting others. Of course, it is also true that achievement does not have to be understood as seeking traditional American values such as wealth and status. There are other possible goals that an individual might want to pursue such as wisdom, creative works, peace of mind, good health, self-appreciation, and friendships. But regardless of whether the individual chooses goals such as these or more traditional ones, it is still possible to see them as contributing to the welfare of others. Achievement can then be defined in a way that entails benevolence. For instance, wealth in this sense is thought of as an instrument to benefit the lives of others.

However, accepting this approach does not mean that one must think in terms of excluding all benefits for oneself from the notion of achievement. No doubt there are several legitimate forms of personal benefit that can result from one's own achievement including the pride of advancement, the reward of sharing what one has attained, and even the enjoyment that comes from experiencing what one has acquired. Following this definition does mean that contributing to the lives of others becomes a significant part of achievement. Personal advancement is thought of as not only reaching something for one's own sake but also of being able to provide something for others.

Another perspective toward achievement and its relationship to benevolence is to think of benevolence as an object of achievement. In this case, benevolence toward others is something that the person seeks to achieve.

This is a constructive viewpoint for the individual as long as benevolence is not separated from other possible objects and is not relegated to an inferior position. That is, it is necessary to think of benevolence as being connected with the other objects in that other goals such as wealth and wisdom must be thought of as necessary to aid others. A dichotomy must be avoided such that the person at times seeks benevolence and at other times seeks some other value which is not associated with benevolence.

In addition, from this viewpoint benevolence must be afforded enough prominence so as to prevent it from being overpowered by a desire for personal gain. It is possible to acknowledge the importance of benevolence being joined with one's other aims but at the same time fail in making it strong enough to be effective. When this occurs, the attainment of other goals may serve as an instrument for benevolent deeds, but these deeds would usually be infrequent and even inconsequential. For example, one's daily vocation might be approached with a desire to be benevolent toward others along with other possible goals of job security, making a substantial salary, obtaining an important ranking in the institution, and being appreciated by others. If benevolence is given an extremely low priority in relation to these other goals, then it will not play a significant role in the individual's job relationships. There will not be the willingness to make the effort often required to assist others.

Thus, achievement should be regarded as being accompanied by benevolence. It should be thought of either as a means toward being benevolent or as having benevolence as a high priority goal closely associated with other goals. If achievement is understood as having this close relationship with benevolence, then it is necessary to explore more carefully the meaning of benevolence. What is the nature of this benevolence that should accompany achievement? One characteristic is that sometimes it is willing to permit suffering to occur. As C. S. Lewis points out, there is a form of kindness that always wants to avoid suffering regardless of the circumstances. This type of kindness does not care whether its object becomes good or bad as long as it escapes suffering.[15] Certainly this is not kindness in the true sense. Genuine benevolence does allow others to suffer if it is necessary for their personal development and understanding. In fact on some occasions it may have to initiate suffering for another either as some kind of physical pain or in the form of mental suffering such as anxiety or embarassment. Benevolence, for instance, may at some point require that an individual be physically restrained and at other times it may demand that someone be confronted about misleading statements or dishonest behavior.

This benevolence also carries with it a willingness to sacrifice. The benevolent individual is able to give up various pursuits toward achievement or at least to postpone them for a period of time. The actions of parents can be an example of this behavior when they decline a more lucrative or prestigious job in order to have more time with their children. Another example of this may be the college student who temporarily drops out of school to assist in the family business. An additional instance of this choice is the management official who has to sacrifice a higher position in the company because of an effort to improve salaries and labor conditions for the workers. Such examples illustrate the sacrificial nature of genuine benevolence.

Even though this benevolence is willing to sacrifice certain achievement oriented activities when necessary, there still remains the recognition of the value of at least some forms of achievement. For one thing, achievement makes an important contribution to human life. All people need a sense of achievement in order to promote their self-fulfillment and self-esteem. As Leo Buscaglia says,

> . . . man needs a feeling of achievement. We all do. We've got to be able to be recognized for doing something well. And somebody's got to point it out to us. Somebody has got to come up occasionally and pat us on the shoulder and say, "That's good. I really like that."[16]

Furthermore, achievement is valuable in that it can serve to enhance benevolence. Some types of achievement can provide a basis for a better means of assisting others and also enable an individual to serve a larger range of people. For instance, the acquisition of knowledge and practical skills in health care, teaching, and church ministry can result in a higher level of benevolence toward others, and the attainment of wealth along with financial power and influence can be used to benefit many people.

Hence, when properly defined, achievement and benevolence are reconcilable concepts and should both be affirmed. Achievement and benevolence should be viewed as being in interaction with each other in the sense that benevolence is involved in the efforts of achievement and achievement contributes to the acts of benevolence. The acceptance of this approach does not mean that conflicts between the two will no longer arise, for there are still decisions to be made in particular situations about which concept should receive the stronger emphasis along with choices about when and how sacrifices should be carried out. However, because there is the understanding that both of these concepts have value and that they are interrelated, the adoption of this outlook should mean that the individual is better prepared to make these decisions.

NOTES

1. Richard Huber, *The American Idea of Success* (New York: McGraw-Hill, 1971) 1–9, 448–57.
2. Ibid., 1–9.
3. Ibid.
4. Ibid., 448–57.
5. Ibid., 449.
6. Daniel Yankelovich, *New Rules, Searching for Self-Fulfillment in a World Turned Upside Down* (New York: Random House, 1981) 72–78, 111–14, 151–52.
7. Ibid., 244–46.
8. Ibid., 174–77.
9. Huber, 448–57.
10. Philip Slater, *The Pursuit of Loneliness.* (Boston: Beacon Press, 1970) 9–10.
11. Erich Fromm, *To Have or To Be?* (New York: Bantam Books, 1976) 57.
12. Ibid., 12–15, 57–65.
13. Peter Singer, "Famine, Affluence, and Morality," *Philosophy and Contemporary Issues.* ed. John Burr and Milton Goldinger (New York: Macmillan, 1984) 219–20.
14. Ibid.
15. C. S. Lewis, *The Problem of Pain* (New York: Macmillan, 1962) 40–41.
16. Leo Buscaglia, *Living, Loving, and Learning* (New York: Ballantine Books, 1982) 55.

DISCUSSION QUESTIONS

1. Are there norms, values, and practices in American society which support and encourage the cultural concept of success? If so, what specific ones are you able to mention?

2. Is it possible to accept both the cultural and personal concepts of success and still maintain a consistent life-style? Do the differences between the two concepts force a person to emphasize one more than the other?

3. Do you think Daniel Yankelovich is correct in claiming that Americans are increasingly emphasizing self-fulfillment and accompanying values such as personal freedom and creativity? What examples are you aware of which would support your view on this question?

4. How do you define success in your own life?

5. Determine which of the following values take priority in the selection and practice of your own vocation: money, material possessions, prestige, self-fulfillment, assisting other people, and service to God. Are there others that you would include?

6. What are some ways in which the American competitive emphasis has made a positive contribution to individuals and society as a whole? In what ways has it been detrimental?

7. What is the difference between an act of duty and an act of charity? Are you aware of any examples of acts in American society that are regarded as charities but which you think ought to be considered duties?

8. Do you think an institution should ever force retirement on an employee before retirement age has been reached? If so, what would be the circumstances in which this is justified?

9. What criteria should be used by persons in professions such as medicine and law in determining the fees that will be charged for different services? Should the determining factor be the acceptable rate in the profession? Do you think that in certain situations these professionals ought to be willing to reduce their charges or even cancel them altogether?

10. What are some situations in which it might be necessary for college students to sacrifice or postpone their efforts toward achievement in order to carry out benevolent acts?

CASE STUDIES

1. Ron and Bob are friends in the same college algebra class. It is the night before a major exam, and both are studying for it. Ron understands the material, but he realizes that he needs to spend a considerable amount of time working problems and reviewing in order to do well on the test. On the other hand, Bob is having difficulty comprehending the basic concepts that need to be learned, and he asks Ron to help him. Ron knows that it will require a great deal of time for him to explain the material to Bob in an adequate manner. He also is aware that helping Bob would give him less time to do his own studying which would probably mean that he would not do as well on the test. What would you do if you were confronted by the decision that Ron faces? Why?

2. Jane and Kay have been college roommates for two years. Jane's parents have recently had some financial setbacks, and they have told her that they will no longer be able to pay for her education. Even though Jane works, she knows that this does not provide her with enough money to cover all of her college expenses. Jane informs Kay that all of her efforts to get enough money to stay in school have failed and that she will not be able to return the next semester. Kay begins to think about her own circumstances and wonders if she should offer to help Jane. Kay's parents have always paid for her education so she is able to use the money that she earns to buy some extra things that she wants. She has about a thousand dollars which she has been planning to use to buy a new record player and some additional clothes. Do you think that Kay should offer to give or loan Jane the money that she has? Would you say that it is Kay's duty to do this?

3. Tom Jensen is the pastor of a middle-class church with a membership of about 750 people. He has been asked by an adult Sunday School department to teach the book of Genesis in the department for the next three months. He realizes that there are several prominent church leaders in the department who have recently been highly critical of him for defending certain nontraditional ideas. He also knows that in many cases his own personal views in interpreting Genesis are quite different from those of most of the people in the department. He wonders what he should do. He feels a responsibility to teach the class and to help the people have a better understanding of the book. He also wants to build good relationships with the people and avoid disagreements in the church whenever possible. What do you think he should do? Should he accept the invitation? If he accepts the invitation should he discuss interpretations of the book that he knows are opposed by a large majority of the people? Should he set forth his own views about the book?

SUGGESTIONS FOR FURTHER READING

Buscaglia, Leo. *Living, Loving and Learning.* New York: Ballantine Books, 1982.
Fromm, Erich. *To Have or To Be?* New York: Bantam Books, 1976.
Huber, Richard. *The American Idea of Success.* New York: McGraw-Hill, 1971.
Lasch, Christopher. *The Culture of Narcissism.* New York: Warner Books, 1979.
Schumacher, E. F. *Small is Beautiful.* New York: Harper and Row, 1973.
Sider, Ron. *Rich Christians in an Age of Hunger.* New York: Paulist Press, 1977.
Yankelovich, Daniel. *New Rules: Searching for Self-Fulfillment in a World Turned Upside Down.* New York: Random House, 1981.

CHAPTER 3
PRIVATE INTERESTS AND THE PUBLIC GOOD

A similar pair of values to achievement and benevolence is that of private interests and the public good. Private interests are the personal concerns that we have for our own lives along with the goals that we are striving to reach. Of course, in our society achievement is often one of the goals that is being sought.

The public good refers to the general welfare, or in other words, what is best for the whole society. Acts that support the public good are often benevolent, but they are not always benevolent for everyone. In some cases these acts are better described as being restrictive or even punitive, at least for part of the population.

Efforts to uphold the public good can call for decisions which contain conflicts between what benefits the whole society and what benefits the individual. This chapter explores certain areas of life where this type of conflict frequently takes place. It first examines the conflict within the family and in the fields of business and politics and then investigates the part it plays in the social issues of ecology and income distribution. The last section of the chapter is a discussion of several basic questions that arise as a person attempts to reconcile private interests and the public good.

The Family

One of the locations of decisions concerning personal interests and the common good is the family. The family serves as the context for the consideration of many of the questions of this nature. It is so often within the family that ideas are discussed and decisions are made which pertain to this conflict. At the same time, in families with children, parents serve as models for how to approach these questions. They demonstrate to children the way that these issues are to be perceived and the specific actions that are to be carried out.

Some examples of these questions within the family are how to vote on tax measures and candidates for public office, whether to support community projects, and if one should be completely honest on income tax forms.

On these issues, it is usually difficult in our society for a person to give attention to the public good on a consistent basis. Because of the social emphasis upon getting ahead and protecting oneself, along with the handy excuse that this is what others do, a strong tendency is present to turn away from thinking of the good of the whole community. It becomes easy to perceive issues from a narrow perspective and to concentrate primarily upon bettering one's own circumstances.

Furthermore, a self-interested attitude within the family has recently become more widespread. Over the past several years a significant number of people have turned more to their families to satisfy their needs and to a larger degree have separated themselves and their families from the outside world. These families have moved closer to being isolated units of society and, simultaneously, have become more inclined to ignore consideration of the public good. Efforts are concentrated more on the welfare of the family and less on the overall good of society.

S. D. Gaede discusses this attitude and refers to it as the illusion of the self-fulfilling family.[1] It grows out of a feeling of insecurity in the midst of the problems of society and is especially a result of the fear of divorce and the breakdown of the family structure. The response is a natural one of huddling together for defense and preservation and one which can be constructive. It, for example, can lead families to maintain cherished values or to cooperate in reaching worthwhile goals. But in today's society it is not unusual for the response to be destructive because the family becomes absorbed in itself. Family members become preoccupied with each other and their own concerns and tend to neglect outward interaction and any sort of community responsibility.

When this unhealthy approach to the family is present, the family is viewed as being of ultimate importance, and everything centers around it. It is assumed that all of a person's relational needs can be met within the family; consequently, it is thought that it is not particularly necessary to develop relationships with other people or become involved in social groups. However, as Gaede insists, this outlook definitely has its weaknesses. Certainly it is true that the family can be an important source of love, fellowship, and belonging, but its provision of these experiences should not be expected to be sufficient in itself. To have this expectation of the family is to be unrealistic and to overburden it with responsibilities. As Gaede says,

> . . . the nuclear family cannot meet all our needs nor is it supposed to. The husband needs relationships with other men; wives need relationships with other women; children need relationships with other children. Moreover, all of them need relationships with the elderly, singles, neighbors, work partners, the poor, and extended—family members—not to mention members of

the local church. The nuclear family is (by historical standards) an extremely narrowly defined entity. As a result, it is well suited to meet the relational needs of parents and children, but ill equipped to handle the variety of other relationships for which we are also responsible[2]

In addition, this family attitude can lead to neglect of other institutions in society and to undermining their importance. Groups such as the government, church, and neighborhood may be misunderstood and their functions may be depreciated and avoided. Also, an attitude of this nature typically results in every activity being evaluated primarily in terms of how it will affect the family. Different decisions relating to one's occupation, religious involvement, and political preferences are made predominantly on the basis of their consequences for the family. It is no doubt the case that the family should be a factor in these decisions, but this approach always gives it priority and therefore downplays other factors.

Finally, this approach to the family usually includes a highly exclusive outlook. These families tend to isolate themselves in neighborhoods with others of similar viewpoints and to avoid interaction with those who are different from themselves. They want, for instance, to stay away from persons who are poor or disadvantaged. They may be interested in becoming aware of such people as well as gaining information about the different problems in society, but only for the sake of the family. This knowledge is used as a means of enabling the family to escape what could prove troublesome.

Television has often been used by these families as an instrument for their purposes. News programs and documentaries provide knowledge of the social diversity and issues in the culture around them. However, this understanding does not lead these family members to involvement in society or to efforts to improve public conditions and the circumstances of those less fortunate than themselves. Rather, it serves as a basis for maintaining personal privacy and avoiding contact with situations and individuals that are regarded as bothersome and which might make some demand upon them.

BUSINESS

Questions about private interests and the public good also arise within the field of business. One of these refers to how employees relate to their companies, such as in the use of company resources, the handling of expense accounts, and the management of their time at work. These decisions concern personal interests in a direct fashion in that employees are making choices based on their own desires, values, and goals. However, they also pertain indirectly to the common good because they have an effect upon the way a business functions in society. Institutions with employees who generally interact with their company in an ethical and efficient manner find it much easier to maintain a high level of operation than do those which are especially lacking in employees who act responsibly. Businesses with an extensive amount of narrow self-interest by members in these company relationships may have difficulty in adequately serving the public and in some cases may not even be able to continue functioning.

Another decision within business institutions concerning private interests and the public good is one that has received considerable attention in recent years under the heading of how a business perceives its social responsibility. This issue concerns decisions made by representatives of business firms on behalf of their companies and has a more direct reference to the public good than does the question of how employees interact with their company. Management officials must determine the consideration that they will give in their plans and operations to their overall relation to society. They have to decide about product quality and safety, environmental protection, employment opportunities, and contributions to social improvement programs.

Allegiance to private interest would be defined more in terms of maximizing profits and production, but of course it should be remembered that the pursuit of this maximization is not necessarily simply a matter of satisfying self-interests. Seeking to increase profits and production can be thought of by business managers as contributing to society, and indeed it often does. It can bring about a stronger business, which in turn can result in many benefits to society. Greater profits and production can mean more jobs, higher wages, better working conditions, increased dividends for stockholders, advanced and diversified products, and expanded forms of service. Therefore, the question here becomes one of whether businesses should think of helping society solely in respect to establishing and maintaining a strong organization. To what extent, if any, are businesses responsible for assisting the public good in ways that go beyond being profitable and perhaps on some occasions run counter to it?

A significant issue at this point pertains to the way that the business itself is to be viewed. Harold Gram is correct in arguing that businesses are not merely economic units which perform only economic activities.[3] They are also social systems consisting of people working together and reacting with each other, their culture, and in some cases the world community. Business institutions produce not only goods and services for the general population but also social satisfactions for the people connected with them. They provide opportunities for creativity, social contacts, new experiences, professional development, and public involvement. Therefore, because of this social role, businesses should not be guided completely by the economic standards of efficiency, profit, and output.

Even when businesses are perceived as social as well as economic, it is still possible to restrict narrowly one's object of concern as a result of a sense of devotion to one's institution or vocation. That is, loyalty is a factor in this issue. Should one's supreme loyalty be to the vocation and institution in which one works? In our society there is a temptation to get caught up in one's own institution and vocation and to lose sight of the general welfare. Frequently a strong competitive element exists between institutions, and employees are called upon to value their own institutions and the particular functions that these organizations have in society. Also, many misunderstandings, prejudices, and hostile attitudes are present within our society toward various vocations and institutions, which brings about alienation and the feeling by members that they must protect themselves and stand up for others of their own kind. Consequently, activities such as unethical competitive practices, deception of the public, and corporate espionage may be thought of as necessary and fully justified.

Regardless of the reasons, the fact remains that it is easy to exaggerate institutional and vocational loyalty in our country and thereby not give proper attention to the public good. Certainly institutional and vocational loyalty is worthwhile and should be upheld, but it should not be affirmed to the extent that the common good is overlooked or depreciated. Loyalty in the sense of an attitude of moral responsibility to the good of society should be at least as strong as institutional and vocational loyalty. Of course, ideally one's loyalty in this regard should not exist in a segmented manner. Institutional and vocational loyalty should be thought of as being intertwined with loyalty for the public good. After all, when vocations and institutions operate properly, they do not rigidly separate the pursuit of goals of their own advancement, the welfare of their employees, and the common good. These are understood to be values which exist together and interact in a dynamic fashion.

Thus, whether businesses are local, national, or international in their outreach, they have a social as well as an economic dimension, and it is necessary for their managers and other employees to have a sense of loyalty that includes a high level of dedication to the public good. It follows that businesses do have an obligation to assist the public good in a manner that transcends simply maintaining a strong institution through increasing profits and the production of goods and services. However, a further question at this point concerns the meaning of this obligation. W. L. LaCroix indicates that two possible social obligations for businesses must be considered.[4] One is what businesses do to society, which involves the impact upon society from the functions of the business itself and includes product quality and safety and environmental pollution. The other possible social obligation for businesses pertains to what businesses could do for society and involves the possible actions by businesses in response to social conditions which are not the effects of business operations. Included are caring for the poor, giving to charities, endowing colleges, and funding cultural programs.

Certainly it can be said that businesses are responsible for what they do to society. They have an obligation to control their activities so that they do not cause unnecessary harm to the general public. Steps must be taken by businesses to prevent such damaging practices as manufacturing unsafe products and polluting the environment. Businesses should design products like automobiles and toys with more care to the overall welfare of the consumer instead of placing so dominant an emphasis upon whether they will be an economic success. Also, industries must be willing to protect the environment by installing the proper pollution control devices and by taking the necessary precautions in disposing of their wastes. It is true that we now have laws as well as designated governmental agencies to uphold product safety and environmental protection. However, these laws do not cover all ways that the public welfare can be abused, and furthermore they are not necessarily always obeyed or enforced. It would be more effective if businesses would concentrate more on thinking of the general welfare and therefore regulate themselves.

An additional question that arises in regard to the impact businesses have on society concerns the issue of unemployment. Do companies have a right to lay off whomever they choose and sometimes to cause widespread unemployment in a community? No doubt situations occur when a company must cut back on its number of employees and at times may even have to make drastic reductions. But even under these circumstances businesses must not abandon their responsibility to the general public. Companies should always be concerned with the effect that their employment reductions have on the particular individuals involved as well as society in general. Even during difficult economic circumstances, business firms should remain sensitive to the general welfare and try to avoid unemployment levels which result in severe hardships for the people.

The other possible social responsibility of businesses is what they could do for society. Do businesses have an obligation to help deal with social issues that are not the result of their own activities? Businesses do not have as strong an ethical obligation here as they do in avoiding unnecessary harm to society from their own actions. Nevertheless, businesses do seem to have a degree of responsibility at this point. As W. L. LaCroix says, businesses are part of the social structure in which they function.[5] Both the businesses and their employees benefit from the social system and the quality of life that is present. Consequently, it seems to follow that businesses have a responsibility to promote the well-being of society and to assist in combating its problems.

How can businesses contribute to society? One way would be directly financial. Businesses obviously could give money to worthy groups such as charities, colleges, museums, and libraries, but they also could provide funds for more specific circumstances like disaster victims (fires, floods, etc.), poverty cases, and those needing college scholarships. Another approach for businesses to assist society would be more educational in intent. Representatives of companies could speak at schools and clubs in their particular field of expertise, and businesses could organize and sponsor educational programs for the community. A further way for businesses to contribute to society would be more humanitarian and cultural in scope. Businesses could aid in sponsoring athletic teams, musical groups, scouting programs, and drama presentations.

POLITICS

A further location for decisions about private interests and the public good is in the realm of politics. Like individuals within businesses, politicians must make decisions which pertain directly to their own self-interests. They must decide to what degree the advancement of their own circumstances and concerns will be a factor in the approaches and measures which they accept. Politicians must determine what effect their supporters, financial and otherwise, will have upon their views. To what extent, will they practice favoritism and reciprocity in their political activities? They must also decide about the impact that the majority viewpoint will have upon their ideas. Should they take a different position from the majority when they think it is beneficial to the general welfare to do so?

Mark Hatfield, longtime United States Senator from Oregon, warns about how the pursuit of power and honor can easily become the primary motivation for the politician. He says that politicians always have available certain persuasive rationalizations to discount the existence of self-interested motives, such as insisting that one's commitment is really serving one's constituents, fighting for justice, or making America more humane. But it is rare to see politicians jeopardize their political careers for the sake of a principle. He points out that as time passes the politician becomes convinced that compromises are necessary for achieving certain goals. In the process, however, means seem to become ends, and there readily develops the domination of the need for self-maintenance.[6]

Hatfield insists that Richard Nixon's efforts to protect his ego and position during the Watergate scandal should not be treated as an isolated incident. In reference to Nixon's situation he asks,

But how different were his pride and ambition from that of most other politicians? Watergate, commonly assumed to be the result of one individual's personal corruption, in actuality went far deeper, revealing the corrupting lust for power that characterizes our entire political system. Countless individuals in public life today, if confronted with the same situation as Richard Nixon, would have acted very much as he did.[7]

Currently the American people have a high degree of disenchantment with the moral character of politicians. No doubt this disenchantment originated to a great extent with the Watergate scandal, but since that time there have been other publicized instances of questionable activities on the part of well-known political figures. More recently several situations have occurred which have raised the level of disillusionment. The problems, for instance, in the personal lives of Gary Hart and John Tower gained national attention and prevented them from achieving the offices which they were seeking. Also, extensive publicity was given to the forced resignations of Tony Coelho from the House of Representatives and Jim Wright as Speaker of the House. Both resignations resulted from improprieties in business dealings and acceptance of gifts.

Is this disenchantment also directed toward state and local politicians? It appears that it usually is, and in many instances the disillusionment is even stronger. Of course, part of the difficulty on these levels has resulted from inefficiency. Town councils, school boards, and state legislatures sometimes have been unwilling to address crucial problems adequately and have been too slow at setting up guidelines or enacting legislation. However, even in these areas there has been a considerable degree of distrust toward politicians. Awareness of political corruption on these levels has also increased in the last two decades. Many cases of bribery, favoritism, the misappropriation of funds, and personal misconduct have been documented and publicized in state and local governments.

Certainly it is unfair to assume that all or even a majority of the politicians in our country are corrupt. We must not stereotype all the members of the political realm as being guilty of unethical practices simply because some are. Yet there is enough evidence to be concerned about the state of politics in our society. Too many politicians have become overly involved with their own narrow self-interests. They have allowed their desire for power, wealth, and a comfortable life-style to acquire too prominent a position in their thinking and behavior. Undoubtedly such a strong emphasis on personal interests serves to restrict their ability to perceive and protect the welfare of all of those they represent.

What would help bring about improvements? What could we as citizens do to better the quality of politics in our society? First we have to avoid becoming captivated by pessimism and cynicism toward the political system. We must refuse to concur with the thinking that says that politicians are necessarily corrupt and inept and cannot be different. Instead of allowing ourselves to become resigned to the current practices in politics, we must insist upon integrity, competence, and diligence from political officials and try to promote progress toward that end even though it may be slow and difficult.

Furthermore, the political system could be improved if more people would become constructively involved. Involvement does not require seeking public office, but it does demand taking an interest in the political process on all levels. We must strive to be aware of the contemporary issues and to participate in discussions and the decision-making processes. We must also support and encourage candidates who have both the ability to lead and a high moral character and who are not simply dedicated to a few private interest groups, but are concerned with the betterment of all of their constituents.

Thus, politiicans must make daily decisions affecting their character and careers which involve the conflict between private interests and the public good. However, this conflict also occurs for politicians in a related but somewhat different sense as they develop and endorse a political philosophy. They must decide about the degree to which their ideology will concentrate upon the advancement of their own kind. To what extent, if any, will their philosophy show preferences for such concerns as their own income level, social status, vocational affiliation, and section of the country? At the same time, they must resolve the question of how much emphasis they will give in their ideas for improvement of those different from themselves and to the well-being of the general population. Of course, in our country citizens also participate in government through voting and in their interchange with others including their representatives; consequently, the conflict is not unique to the politician. Citizens also develop an overall political outlook along with views about specific issues, and in the process they must make decisions about personal interests and the good of the whole society.

Arthur Schlesinger, Jr., argues that since the beginning of our society there have been cycles in the political philosophy and practices of the American people. Each of these cycles has lasted approximately thirty years with the two phases of a cycle lasting about fifteen years each. These continuing cycles represent shifts over the years in the national mood between private interest and public purpose. These shifts are not determined by external events such as war, depression, and inflation, but rather are explained by internal events with each new phase growing out of the conditions of the preceding phase.[8]

The eras of self-interest are characterized by materialism and a quest for personal gratification and privacy. They set forth the principle that promoting one's own interest also promotes the general interest, and they assume that the best way to deal with public problems is to let the market operate in an independent fashion. During these periods, typically a call is set forth for *laissez-faire*, and a crusade against government regulation and taxes is promoted. Eventually, however, says Schlesinger, people get bored with selfish motives and materialsim and begin to seek meaning in life beyond themselves. Consistent with the advice of John F. Kennedy, they begin to ask what they can do for their country instead of what it can do for them, which soon leads into the period of seeking public good. It is characterized by social involvement and a desire to improve the entire society and emphasizes action, passion, idealism, and reform. But after awhile people become disillusioned by the results, and they also get tired because sustained public action can be exhausting. They seek a time of rest and recuperation, and they desire to pursue the privacies of life, which leads, therefore, to a recurrence of the stage of self-interest.[9]

Furthermore, Schlesinger contends that a feedback exists from the generation in power to the generation arriving at political consciousness. That is, the generations in their late teens and early twenties tend to have their political philosophy shaped by the events and ideals that are dominant at the time. As a result, each new generation that reaches power reenacts the ideals of its formative years about thirty years before. Additionally, this process of structuring political values is reinforced by an individual's association with family members. Because of the time differential, people often come to political consciousness under the same political emphasis as that which shaped their parents and grandparents. Consequently, the influence of parents and grandparents usually serves as a further impetus for the individual toward those ideals that are prominent during their early adulthood.[10]

It is interesting to relate Schlesinger's views to our contemporary circumstances. Certainly the Reagan era of the 1980s was generally consistent with his description of the period of self-interest. The decade of the '80s was especially a time when personal gratification and privacy were strongly emphasized, and the Reagan administration did indeed seek to minimize taxation and the government regulation of businesses. Along with these policies, it is interesting to note that the start of the 1990s marks thirty years since the 1960s, and the '60s in many ways represented an era of social involvement and seeking the public good. The civil rights movement and the Viet Nam protests exemplified the spirit of action, passion, idealism, and reform. Furthermore, it should be noted that many of the leaders in our country who are now in their forties or fifties were strongly influenced by the philosophy of the 1960s. They were young adults when the events of '60s were taking place.

The obvious question is whether the decade of the 1990s will produce a recognizable turn toward seeking the public good. Will there be a transition into a period heavily characterized by social involvement and efforts to improve society? Certainly our country could benefit from such a transition. We have a desperate need for action and/or reform in environmental protection, poverty and the welfare program, the income tax structure, and the health care system. However, whether or not this transition actually occurs during the '90s, hopefully during this time, these problems will be seriously addressed so that progress can be made toward their correction.

THE ENVIRONMENT

The conflict between private interests and the public good also arises within certain social issues, including various concerns related to the environment and the question of income distribution. The environment is a rather broad category with numerous topics. One is the pollution of the environment, which can be discussed in terms of the basic divisions of water, air, and land. Unfortunately each of these areas is presently suffering from a large amount of abuse, and each has some serious problems associated with it.

Every year our oceans have over seven million tons of petroleum products added to them, coming not only from accidental spillage from ships but also from river and urban runoff and the routine discharges of tankers as they are cleaned. The worst cause of inland water pollution in the United States is topsoil erosion, which results especially from careless agricultural practices, but logging, mining, and construction are also contributors. Water pollution in our country has many other causes such as human and animal sewage, pesticides, salt from the deicing of roads, food processing industries, electric power plants, and industrial wastes. These sources add oil, metals, plastics, salt, radioactive substances, and various chemicals to our waterways, and these pollutants sometimes find their way into the drinking water supplies of American cities. Contaminated drinking water is a growing problem in the United States.[11]

The major sources of air pollution are automobile exhausts, cigarette smoking, and wastes from industries such as pulp and paper mills, iron and steel mills, petroleum refineries, and chemical plants. On the average the troposphere (the zone extending five to seven miles above the earth's surface) now receives about 548,000 tons of air pollutants from the United States (other nations are also polluting) each day. This continuous and massive pollution of the air Americans breathe is directly injuring our health. Diseases of the heart and blood vessels in the United States have increased in this century, probably to some extent because of the rise in the levels of carbon monoxide and sulfate particles that we inhale. Carbon monoxide deprives the body of oxygen and contributes to headaches, fatigue, impaired judgment, and a greater workload for the heart. Respiratory diseases such as bronchial asthma, bronchitis, and emphysema have increased in this century. Emphysema, for instance, is now the fastest growing cause of death in the country. In addition to the adverse effect that air pollution has on human health, it is also harming other parts of the environment. Acid rain, for example, which results from the formation of sulfuric and nitric acid in the atmosphere, has become a serious threat to other forms of life. It has already damaged crops and trees and killed most of the aquatic life in certain lakes.[12]

Our land is polluted by the discarding of solid wastes which come from numerous sources, including animals, industries, mining, and municipal garbage. The yearly output of animal manure in this country is approximately the same as the wastes of two billion humans. About half of this is spread back on the land, but the rest is a potential threat to surface and ground water. A significant portion of the industrial wastes are toxic or in some sense hazardous. The Environmental Protection Agency has estimated that only about ten percent of our hazardous and toxic wastes are disposed of properly with the rest serving as a risk to human health and the environment.[13]

Another topic within the environmental issue is the use of nonrenewable and renewable resources. The United States consumes a large percentage of the world's nonrenewable resources (coal, petroleum, and minerals). We, for instance, use about one-third of the world's production of minerals. The fundamental problem is that the amount of these resources is limited and that some of them are already in short supply. Furthermore, with the constant rise in the world's population, many of them are being depleted at an increasing rate. Environmentalists are insisting that we must move toward practicing conservation of nonrenewable resources and relying more on renewable resources. In the future one possibility in this regard is in the production of energy. It is suggested that we learn to depend on renewable sources of energy like water power, solar power, wind energy, and biomass energies (burning wood, animal wastes, etc.).[14]

A further subject concerning the environment is overpopulation. There were about 1.6 billion people in the world at the beginning of this century, and by mid-century there were 2.5 billion people on earth. By 1986 the world population figure had doubled to reach 5 billion, and by the year 2000 it is expected to reach over 6 billion. Even though the rate of population growth has fallen over the past decade, the net absolute annual addition to the number of people is increasing. It is projected that this addition will increase from about 78 million per year at present to about 90 million per year by 2000.

The large majority of growth is occurring in poorer, developing countries with African nations expanding at the fastest rate. It is expected, for instance, that in the next thirty years the population of Kenya will grow from 23 million to 79 million and the population of Nigeria will rise from 112 million to 274 million. The annual growth rate is not as high in India and China, but they still have huge increases of population each year because of their large existing populations.

Substantial increases in population translate into a strain on the environment and on the economic and social well-being of the people. Problems have emerged especially in the poorest countries with resources being depleted, grasslands being overgrazed, and forests being destroyed for fuel and more farmland. The past decade has witnessed increasing instances of starvation in parts of Africa, Asia, and South America along with a steady decline for many in basic living conditions. A growing number of people in the world have inadequate access to food, water, shelter, sanitation, and health care.

Hence, the environmental issue includes the topics of pollution, the use of resources, and overpopulation. The conflict between private interest and the public good in relation to environmental questions results both from group participation and individual situations. For example, we may have to decide whether we will support the institution for which we work when it extensively engages in polluting the environment or wasting resources. Also, in our personal lives we may have to make choices concerning the use of the environment and whether we are willing to use renewable resources even though they may be more expensive or less convenient than nonrenewable ones. Additionally, there are questions about whether we will encourage government aid for poverty stricken countries and make individual contributions to worthy groups working in these areas.

What are some ideas and guidelines that would provide a constructive means of approaching environmental questions and dealing with the conflicts? One is simply a greater awareness of the relationship between humanity and the rest of nature. Our society needs to have a better understanding of the various ways that human beings are dependent upon both the organic and inorganic phases of nature and how our well-being is closely associated with theirs. A greater knowledge of the interdependence of all existing things would help to increase the value that we place on the other parts of nature as well as aid us in becoming more environmentally conscious in our actions. In recent years there have been some improvements on these matters as a result of the efforts of public education and other sources, but hopefully in the future more emphasis will be given in this direction so that the improvements will grow and be more widespread.

Second, we should seek to discourage greed and envy not only in our own lives but also throughout American society. E. F. Schumacher says that Americans have been caught up in pursuing economic progress and have cultivated the qualities of greed and envy as a means of reaching this goal. This constant stress upon these qualities has brought about a collapse of intelligence so that it is difficult for us to see things as they really are. He says that it is this distortion of reality which is at the basis of our misuse of the environment. It is hard for us to appreciate the environment which is necessary in order to give it priority and protect it.[15]

Third, we must practice conservation and avoid waste. Albert Fritsch claims that part of the overall need of Americans is to accept a simpler life-style. He says that a simplicity of life-style does not necessarily mean that one must become isolated like a hermit or has to live a plain life without jewelry, decorations, and cosmetics. However, it does mean an absence of waste, luxury, and extravagance and a quality of consciousness in which one strives to conserve the resources of food, water, fossil fuel, and wildlife. It implies less fashion-orientation, less needless travel, less consumption of energy, less addiction to commercialism, more walking, more acts of shar-ing and cooperation with others, and more community participation and control. In terms of specific practices, it includes consuming less meat, encouraging mass transportation, opposing the use of nonreturnable items, supporting the recycling of materials, and reducing water usage in the home.[16]

In addition, Fritsch argues that American society has a duty to formulate laws that restrict the excessive use of resources. He says we recognize the need to restrict antisocial behavior and to prohibit certain actions such as robbery and murder. Robbery is not permitted in our country, and the excessive use of resources borders on robbery. He points out that some are saying that to restrict the use of resources we should rely upon taxation or let the economy control the situation with higher prices for rare resources. Fritsch insists that these means are not adequate, for these procedures do not manage to limit certain groups, particularly the wealthy. We must have specific restrictions that apply to everyone. These laws should be fair in their application, and they should seek to preserve human freedom as much as possible. They also must be accompanied by sufficient penalties to deter a continuous pattern of misuse.[17]

Finally, we should take an active interest in the economic and social problems in other countries. This will include some type of involvement ourselves to assist impoverished countries, such as directly working in these areas or making financial contributions to those who are. It will further include the support of various types of government and private programs that are seeking to improve conditions in these nations. For instance, we should encourage programs which provide birth-control information and devices in these countries and those which are doing research on new birth-control methods that might be easier to use or more acceptable in other cultures.

INCOME DISTRIBUTION

The issue of income distribution is the question of what constitutes a fair distribution of income in American society and to what extent, if any, it should be redistributed. Should the government seek to redistribute income in order to create greater equality of income and wealth among the population? Of course, our society generally assumes that some degree of redistribution is necessary, at least in regard to providing food and financial assistance for the poor. Then the question becomes one of asking how far we should go in redistributing income to achieve greater equality. How much financial aid and other services such as health care, housing, and education should the government provide for the poor and the general population?

One way that income can be redistributed is through government regulations. Our American tradition of *laissez-faire* economics has warned of the detrimental effect that these interventions can have on the overall economy and has insisted that we keep them to a minimum. Nevertheless, possibilities exist that should be recognized and discussed. For instance, should there be a widespread regulation of businesses in order to keep down the prices of products? Also, should restrictions be placed on the fees for certain services such as in the medical and legal professions? Questions such as these have to be given a twofold consideration. One is whether justice is served through intervention by allowing a fairer means of exchange. The other is determining the effect that these regulations will have upon the economy as a whole. It is possible for government action to be self-defeating in the sense of creating greater hardships and injustices than the ones that are overcome.

Another way that income can be redistributed is through taxation and public expenditures. That is, money is taken from the general public by means of taxes and then used by the government to support various programs for society. Here questions arise about how the tax system should be structured and whether it is fair in its requirements. For example, should an effort be made to increase inheritance taxes? Also, should corporations be taxed at a higher rate? Other questions concern how the government spends the money that has been acquired. How much, for instance, should be used on programs for the poor and elderly and how much should be given to military spending?

Thus, income can be redistributed through taxation and government spending as well as through government regulations. Many questions pertaining to this issue have various aspects associated with them which render them extremely complex and difficult to answer. Usually they not only demand insights into the workings of the American economy but also involve decisions about the meaning of justice and the value of the qualities of personal freedom and income equality. Furthermore, they frequently include the conflict between private interests and the public good. Answers to these questions are possible that may aid certain persons and conceivably even society in general, but at the same time these results may go against the personal interests of other groups or individuals. For example, reformulations of the income tax system are possible which would oppose the immediate concerns of the rich, and if limits were placed on fees in some of the vocations, they would be contrary to the private interests of these groups.

In seeking to deal with questions of this nature there are some broad guidelines that are beneficial. One is that it ought to be recognized that to live a full life, all people have a right to a share of the economic products of society. These include rights to a basic level of material goods, to useful employment, and to adequate opportunities of self-development, such as through education and leisure time. Undoubtedly it is difficult to say exactly how far these rights extend, but progress is made by at least acknowledging that each person has some fundamental rights.[18]

In addition, basic principles of economic efficiency serve as guidelines. Even though we may desire a greater sense of justice and equality in the distribution of income in our society, there are certain economic facts that must be remembered. One is, as economist Arthur M. Okun points out, that we must maintain a system of rewards and penalties within our economy which encourages effort and that results in a productive society. That is, we do not want to sanction too many programs that interfere with personal initiative and thereby in the long run harm the individual as well as society. Furthermore, as Okun says, it is possible to hinder the investments of the rich so that the economy is weakened and the quality and quantity of jobs are reduced. In other words, we do not want to restrict the rich to such an extent that we harm the rest of society.[19]

Along with these guidelines, other writers also make several helpful suggestions for approaching these questions. Lester Thurow, an economist, points out that economic growth by itself is not the answer. In the past it has often been assumed that if everyone just had more, then we would not have to address these questions concerning equality and distribution. It has been thought that an increase in income and wealth would make everyone happy, but Thurow insists that happiness does not necessarily follow. An individual's economic situation is a relative matter so that even if one's own wealth increases, it may not produce contentment. If the position of others in other classes in society increases at a greater rate, then the individual may feel deprived and dissatisfied.[20]

Thurow says that a tendency will exist in our society in the future for the gap between the rich and the poor to increase, and we must strive to prevent this discrepancy. Consequently, transfer payments to the poor will have to continue to increase, and a strong tax plan will be necessary to support these payments as well as the other public programs. This plan will have to depend particularly upon the income tax system which at the present time not only does not gather enough revenue but also is grossly unfair. This unfairness is exemplified in the United States by persons with the same income paying different taxes. Also, many wealthy individuals in our country are currently paying little or no income tax. The system is organized in such a way that it offers many loopholes for holders of capital and few loopholes for wage earners. Therefore, in the future the income tax structure must be reformulated both to increase the revenue gained and for the sake of justice. One possibility is to close some of the loopholes and to give more attention to taxing capital instead of concentrating so heavily upon income.[21]

Moreover, a philosopher named John Rawls makes some constructive suggestions for dealing with these questions about income distribution. He contends that if we are seeking a just scheme for the regulation of society, we should select an approach that could be accepted from an impartial stance. Impartiality could be achieved by first pretending that we don't know the position that we now have in society. In other words, he says we should choose our principles with the assumption that we are not aware of our actual circumstances within the system. As a result, our principles would avoid personal biases and incorporate a greater sense of fairness for everyone. Because we would not know whether we would be among the least advantaged, we would definitely want to offer protection for them.[22]

According to Rawls, when this perspective is utilized, we can agree to the basic principle that equal liberties and fair opportunities should be present for each of us. But he says we can also accept what he calls "the difference principle" which means that social and economic inequalities can be justified only if they contribute to raising the position of others in society, especially the least advantaged groups. Those who have gained more must operate in a manner that is beneficial to those who have gained the least, and in Rawls's view the government should adjust its policies to conform to this principle. In regard to taxation, for instance, those at the top should be taxed to the point that it would decrease their contribution to the rest of society to be taxed further.[23]

RESPONSIBILITIES FOR THE PUBLIC GOOD

Decisions regarding private interests and the public good occur in numerous areas of our society including the family, business, politics, and in certain social issues. In making these decisions several basic questions arise concerning the relationship between personal interests and general welfare. One is whether an individual should think in terms of having responsibilities for the public good. Is a person really obligated to promote the welfare of the whole? With the strong individualistic tradition in our society, no doubt a tendency exists to reject these responsibilities or at least relegate them to secondary importance. In our culture the emphasis is placed more upon formulating and pursuing individual goals. Usually the acknowledgment is made that the public good should be upheld, but often it is regarded as someone else's concern. It is considered the responsibility of government officials or various leaders within groups.

Regardless of the nature of popular viewpoints, each individual does have responsibilities to the public good. Furthermore, the term "public" in this context must be interpreted in a broad sense to include many groups and their constituents such as neighborhood, institution of work, and the town and state of residence. It even includes the larger class of mankind in general. To support the public good is to preserve the welfare of each of these groups.

The justification for claiming that people have responsibilities to the public good is similar to the argument insisting that businesses have obligations for social involvement. That is, like businesses all people are a part of the public domain. Each individual participates in the global community as well as a specific vacinity and country; each gains from this participation. We benefit from the order, products, and services that are available around us. Therefore, because we are a part of this larger whole and acquire benefits from it, we have a responsibility to ensure its welfare.

A question that follows concerns the meaning of these responsibilities. What form do these responsibilities take? These responsibilities may be general or particular. General responsibilities of everyone are obeying laws, paying taxes, and protecting the environment. Another general responsibility of each person is assisting in dealing with social problems. Obviously a person cannot be heavily involved in every problem present in society; consequently, issues must be chosen which are most consistent with the individual's interests and circumstances.

A particular responsibility for the public good is one relating to an individual's personal conditions such as occupation, living location, talents, group affiliations, education, relatives, and friends. Certain persons, for instance, because of their leadership roles within their institutions of work, have the special responsibility of steering their organizations toward higher levels of public concern. Another example is that people who are influential in the lives of relatives and friends are responsible for trying to discourage them when they want to abuse the common good.

Thus, each person has both general and particular responsibilities to support the public good. A further question concerns how these responsibilities can be reconciled with a person's private interests. Does the acceptance of these responsibilities imply that private interests must be rejected? It is possible to reconcile these responsibilities with one's own interests, but this demands that these interests must take on a certain form. Obviously not all private interests are consistent with these responsibilities because personal goals and concerns can be directly opposed to the general good. But as Douglas Den Uyl reminds us, personal interests do not have to be antisocial passions.[24] When our interests are grounded in values of justice, equality, and compassion, they will give a high priority to maintaining the general welfare.

Therefore, personal interests and the public good can be reconciled in a way that is similar to the reconciliation of achievement and benevolence. Just as one's concept of achievement must be structured to include benevolence, so also must one's private interests be formulated to recognize the value of the public good. In other words, the good of the whole must be one of the concerns that the individual accepts. Furthermore, it must be a high priority interest for the person. Otherwise, efforts toward the public good will be readily abandoned for the sake of reaching individual goals or acquiring personal gratification.

NOTES

1. S. D. Gaede, *Belonging* (Grand Rapids: Zondervan Publishing House, 1985) 112–15, 120–22.

2. Ibid., 114.

3. Harold Gram, *Ethics and Social Responsibility in Business* (St. Louis: Concordia Publishing House, 1969) 41–42.

4. W. L. LaCroix, *Principles for Ethics in Business* (Washington: University Press of America, 1978) 92–103.

5. Ibid., 104–05.

6. Mark Hatfield, *Between a Rock and a Hard Place* (Waco: Word Books, 1976) 15.

7. Ibid., 15–16.

8. Arthur M. Schlesinger, Jr., *The Cycles of American History* (Boston: Houghton Mifflin Company, 1986) 26–31.

9. Ibid., 28–29, 38–40.

10. Ibid., 30–31, 38–39.

11. John Carmody, *Ecology and Religion: Toward a New Christian Theology of Nature* (New York: Paulist Press, 1983) 13–16.

12. Ibid., 16–19.

13. Ibid., 19–21.

14. Ibid., 30–36.

15. E. F. Schumacher, *Small is Beautiful* (New York: Harper and Row, 1973) 30–34.

16. Albert J. Fritsch, *Environmental Ethics* (Garden City: Doubleday, 1980) 202–21.

17. Ibid., 221–27.

18. Virginia Held, "Introduction," *Property, Profits and Economic Justice,* ed. Virginia Held (Belmont, California: Wadsworth, Inc., 1980) 16–19.

19. Arthur M. Okun, "Rights and Dollars," *Property, Profits and Economic Justice,* ed. Virginia Held (Belmont, California: Wadsworth, Inc., 1980) 221–23.

20. Lester C. Thurow, *The Zero-Sum Society: Distribution and the Possibilities for Economic Change* (New York: Penguin Books, 1980) 16–19.

21. Ibid., 168–78, 193–94.

22. John Rawls, "A Kantian Conception of Equality," *Property, Profits and Economic Justice,* ed. Virginia Held (Belmont, California: Wadsworth, Inc., 1980) 198–206.

23. Ibid.

24. Douglas J. Den Uyl, "Self-Interest and American Ideology," *Ideology and American Experience,* ed. John K. Roth and Robert C. Whittemore (Washington: The Washington Institute Press, 1986) 106–107.

DISCUSSION QUESTIONS

1. Do you think that the preoccupation of the family with itself, which S. D. Gaede discusses, is a serious problem in our country today? Are you aware of examples of this attitude among particular families?

2. Do you think one should seek to be completely honest on income tax forms? Should personal tax breaks be refused if one considers them to be wrong or unfair for society as a whole?

3. Evaluate the following activities in terms of whether you consider them unethical and in what sense they might be harmful to society as a whole: wasting time at work, the personal use of institutional property and supplies, the misuse of an institutional expense account, and charging extremely high fees for professional services.

4. To what extent, if any, do you think businesses have social responsibilities? Should every business donate time or money to help improve society in such areas as crime, drugs, and poverty?

5. Do you think political representatives in our country should vote according to the majority views of their constituents or according to their own individual views?

6. How would you describe the nature of the dominant political philosophy in our country when you first arrived at political consciousness? Would you characterize it as having more emphasis on private interests or upon public purpose? Are you aware of any ways in which you disagree with it?

7. Do you think the American way of life has tended to promote greed and envy as Schumacher contends? What specific suggestions would you have for persons who want to avoid these qualities in their own lives?

8. Do you think each of us should strive for the simpler life-style which Fritsch describes? Are you able to list any other attitudes and practices that might be included in this life-style besides those mentioned in the chapter?

9. Do you think that we need stronger government regulations in our country in regard to

prices of products and fees charged for certain services? If so, what specific areas do you think should be regulated?

10. Do you think that our income tax system needs to be altered? If so, what changes would you suggest?

11. What is your evaluation of John Rawls's suggestions? Do you agree with what he calls "the difference principle"?

12. What are other examples of general responsibilities for the public good besides the ones mentioned in the chapter? What do you think are your own particular responsibilities for the public good?

CASE STUDIES

1. Jay Benson is married and has two children in high school. In the late 1960s Jay borrowed several thousand dollars from the federal government to help him with his college expenses, and he has never repaid the loan. He was supposed to have repaid it years ago, but he always had other expenses and never got around to it. The government is now making a stronger appeal to him for repayment, and he does think he ought to pay it back. He realizes that those who default on their loans hurt the program and make it more difficult for others to obtain loans. But he wonders if now is the proper time for him to return the money. His wife has been ill and has accumulated heavy medical expenses. His children are also getting older and have more expenses. For Jay to repay the loan at the present time would require a great deal of sacrifice on his part. He would have to work many hours of overtime and perhaps even have to get an additional job. What do you think he should do?

2. Jack Handley lives in a small town and has recently gone on a hunting trip with a group of fellow businessmen. A problem that he discovered was that the men quickly became intoxicated to the point that they endangered their own lives as well as those of others. They also exceeded the limit of animals that they were allowed to kill and were cruel in their treatment of animals. They left game on the ground where it fell and sometimes wounded animals for fun. Jack has returned from the trip and is trying to decide what he should do. He attempted to talk to them about the problems while he was on the trip, but that didn't seem to have any effect on their actions. He wonders if he should tell others about what these men do on their hunting trips. Because these are influential men in the town, he knows that by telling others he could easily put his own business and position in society in jeopardy. What do you think he should do?

3. Ben and Sue Sanders are an upper middle-class couple with two children, ages seven and nine. They are trying to decide whether to take their children out of a public school and put them in a private school. On the one hand, they have investigated the private school and think it will be better academically for their children. It doesn't seem to have as many discipline problems, and overall the children seem to be at a higher level of learning. They also think that the private school would offer some social advantages for their children in that the similar socioeconomic backgrounds of the other children would probably make it easier for their children to make friends. On the other hand, the Sanderses are concerned that the private school will not allow their children to experience much diversity in the types of people with whom they interact. They want their children to be able to understand and relate to people who are different from themselves. The Sanderses also wonder about the possible negative effect upon the public schools if a large number of people like themselves put their children in private schools. Furthermore, they ask themselves if it is really fair for some people to be able to go to private schools while others cannot. What do you think the Sanderses should do?

SUGGESTIONS FOR FURTHER READING

Carmody, John. *Ecology and Religion: Toward a New Christian Theology of Nature.* New York: Paulist Press, 1983.

Fritsch, Albert J. *Environmental Ethics.* Garden City: Doubleday, 1980.

Gaede, S. D. *Belonging.* Grand Rapids: Zondervan Publishing House, 1985.

Gram, Harold. *Ethics and Social Responsibility in Business.* St. Louis: Concordia Publishing House, 1969.

Hatfield, Mark. *Between a Rock and a Hard Place.* Waco: Word Books, 1976.

Held, Virginia, ed. *Property, Profits and Economic Justice.* Belmont, California: Wadsworth, Inc., 1980.

LaCroix, W. L. *Principles for Ethics in Business.* Washington: University Press of America, 1978.

Roth, John K. and Whittemore, Robert C. *Ideology and American Experience.* Washington: The Washington Institute Press, 1986.

Schlesinger, Arthur M., Jr., *The Cycles of American History.* Boston: Houghton Mifflin Company, 1986.

Thurow, Lester C. *The Zero-Sum Society: Distribution and the Possibilities for Economic Change.* New York: Penguin Books, 1980.

CHAPTER 4
DETACHMENT AND INVOLVEMENT

The conflict between detachment and involvement concerns the question of whether to extend oneself in a relationship in the outside world. Involvement affirms this outward interaction, but, in contrast, detachment in some sense rejects it. Detachment may take the form of an individual withdrawing into solitary activity like exercising, reading, resting, or reflecting. In these situations there may be a complete absence of involvement with those outside oneself. However, detachment does not always refer to a disengagement from every facet of the external world. It is possible for a person to be detached from a certain aspect of life but to be involved in other areas. An individual, for example, may be largely isolated from community organizations and social issues and yet be highly involved with friends and family members.

This chapter examines the nature of the conflict between detachment and involvement. It points out the main areas of decision regarding this conflict as well as some of the specific questions that arise in each area. The chapter gives special attention to discussing a number of unhealthy responses to detachment and involvement and to describing a more satisfactory approach to these concepts.

AREAS OF DECISION

One of the major categories for decisions about detachment and involvement concerns a person's associations with family members, other relatives, friends, and neighbors. A decision that is prevalent in family relationships pertains to how often one has contact with various relatives. Spouses must make choices about how much time they spend with each other, and young adults must determine when and how often they will return home to visit with their parents. At the same time parents must decide the degree of involvement that they should have with their children. Decisions must be made not only when the children are small but also when they are adolescents and adults. In addition to decisions about the amount of time to be spent, other decisions about the family are included in this conflict. For example, choices must be made about whether or not to give support to other family members in their work and activities by providing financial assistance, attending public performances, and offering guidance and encouragement.

Like one's relationships with family members, the associations with friends, neighbors, and relatives beyond the immediate family also cover decisions about the extent that one interacts with them. One must decide about talking with a neighbor in the yard, calling a friend on the telephone, and inviting relatives to visit. Questions also exist about whether to make sacrifices in these relationships. If neighbors are planning a vacation, for instance, should one volunteer to mow their yard or keep their pet? Should one talk to friends about their personal problems or go to the funeral of one of their family members? When relatives are unemployed, should an extensive effort be made to help them find a job?

The other major area which contains decisions about detachment and involvement is society in general. This area includes community organizations, social issues, vocational activities, and contact with acquaintances, which all produce a variety of questions. Should one offer assistance to an acquaintance who has a problem, and how much time and effort should one put into a job. Choices also must be made about joining a civic group or church and deciding on the degree of involvement. Additionally, there are questions about whether to make specific efforts toward improving society and combating social problems of poverty, drug abuse, environmental pollution, and unjust discrimination. Moreover, when "society" is interpreted in a broad sense, this category includes decisions about relationships with other countries and the rest of humanity. Questions arise about world hunger, apartheid in South Africa, and the dissension and warfare in Central America and the Middle East.

Thus, there are two main areas in which the conflict between detachment and involvement takes place. Of course, even if one decides that an expression of involvement is called for, it may still be difficult to determine the form it should take. How much financial aid, for example, should be offered to a family member? Should one volunteer to carry out all of the local responsibilities of neighbors while they are out of town? What social organizations should a person join and which social problems should be addressed?

Other possible choices should be mentioned. In some circumstances an individual may have to decide which commitment will be given more emphasis. On a weekend home from college, for instance, will a student spend Saturday on a family outing or use the time to be with friends? On a given evening, will a person attend the public activity of a family member or go to a church meeting? Furthermore, there may be decisions about the kind of detachment that will be followed. Even if on a particular occasion a person chooses to become disengaged from all relationships with others, there are still many different forms that the detachment might take. For example, will a student take up physical exercise or seek to read and study? Will a person simply relax and clear the mind or will an attempt be made to reflect and perhaps plan for the future?

However, all of these questions are related to the concepts of detachment and involvement. In seeking to answer these questions, it is of course necessary in each case to consider carefully the circumstances surrounding the decision. There are certainly a variety of combinations of detachment and involvement that may be called for in a person's life according to the particular situations that arise. At times total detachment is appropriate so that solitary activities may be carried out, and other times extensive acts of involvement are needed. As individuals make these decisions they often develop certain general perspectives for dealing with these questions. An overall approach for understanding the various situations and for relating to the different areas of life is acquired. This approach becomes a guideline for making future decisions and in turn gives rise to certain habitual patterns of behavior. Sometimes a pattern of behavior is unhealthy because in some way it does not allow adequate detachment or involvement to take place. That is, there is some sense in which detachment or involvement is not properly emphasized and certain responsibilities of the individual are seriously neglected. This not only is harmful to the individual but also usually has negative repercussions for others as well.

UNHEALTHY INVOLVEMENT

Looking first at efforts of involvement, it is clear that unhealthy possibilities exist. One possibility is to get overly caught up in social involvement through the endeavors of organizations such as a church, club, or special interest group, and another is to become obsessed with the activities of one's own vocation. These forms of involvement are expressions of what has been called workaholism, which Wayne Oates defines as the "addiction to work, the compulsion or the uncontrollable need to work incessantly."[1] It is like alcohol and drug addiction in that it creates disturbances in the normal processes of life; it interferes with bodily health, personal happiness, interpersonal relations, and smooth social functioning. However, workaholism is different from other addictions in that it does not have a social stigma attached to it. It is more socially acceptable than alcohol and drug abuse.[2]

Several factors have contributed to the presence of overwork in the lives of some Americans. A more obvious one is the strong emphasis that our society has traditionally given to diligent work. Our society highly values being perpetually busy and being able to accomplish many tasks. Institutions typically encourage this kind of behavior and offer rewards to those who engage in it. Along with this, working extremely long hours can serve as a source of ego gratification not only in that it can be a means of gaining praise but also in that it can be a way by which people seek to outdo others and reach their goals. Furthermore, in some cases workaholism grows out of religious beliefs such as the Protestant Work Ethic. The person may strongly believe that excessive work is favored by God and that the harder one works the greater are God's blessings. There may even be present a kind of salvation by works in which it is affirmed that in order to gain salvation one must work hard and gain God's acceptance.[3]

Another factor contributing to overwork is that ethical instruction in both social institutions and the home has often largely overlooked one's obligations to oneself. The moral teaching has concentrated more upon one's ethical responsibilities toward other people. As a result, individuals are frequently not fully aware of these personal obligations or at least do not give them the attention that they deserve. Undoubtedly these can be outweighed in importance in many situations by one's obligations toward others, but this does not mean that they should be totally ignored or treated as being of little significance. These duties to oneself have their place in decision making and should be considered along with one's outward responsibilities in the world.

What is the nature of these obligations to oneself? A variety of examples are sometimes referred to as being part of these obligations, but three requirements especially deserve to be mentioned. One pertains to physical demands including proper diet, rest, recreation, and exercise along with the avoidance of unnecessary abuse of the body such as with drugs. There are also requirements regarding the development of one's inward self such as through self-examination, meditation, and prayer. Additionally, there are demands which concern the training and development of one's mental abilities including studying, reading, and listening to informative presentations.

A further factor that has sometimes encouraged workaholism is a kind of inauthentic existence in which there is an inability or unwillingness to make one's own decisions. This may occur for various reasons sometimes because the person may be young and not yet have fully developed a decision-making capacity. Also, there may be a hesitation and a lack of courage on the part of the individual in disagreeing with older persons and authority figures. Moreover, it is possible that the person may wish to avoid the uncertainty and anxiety that so often accompanies making one's own choices. For whatever reasons, the result is that people with this approach let others make decisions for them. In this way they leave themselves open to those who are looking for volunteers for their efforts. Even when these organizers basically have good intentions and their goals are admirable, they are often preoccupied with simply getting workers for their activities and do not give sufficient attention to the overall welfare of those they draft. This frequently leads those who respond in an inauthentic manner to become overextended in involvement endeavors.

In addition to these factors that contribute to excessive work, it should be noted that there is sometimes a tragic sense of irony that accompanies this situation of the workaholic. Of course, not all workaholics are particularly concerned with wanting to improve society. Some are merely interested in working for themselves and achieving prestige and personal goals that they have structured for themselves. Yet, workaholics may be sincerely interested in benefiting society and may especially think of their activities in this manner. When this is the case, it is not unusual for them to want to be drawn closer to others in their relationships and to anticipate that their work will lead them in this direction. The tragedy is that overwork typically results in just the opposite. When people become workaholics, they so often separate themselves from others. They tend to become alienated and isolated and to experience deep feelings of loneliness.

Unhealthy involvement, therefore, may take the form of getting caught up in overwork through social or vocational activities. Is it possible for one to be overly involved with family, friends, or relatives? There is not much attention given to this today because of the current problems of detachment from these areas. However, there are a number of ways that this can take place. For example, parents may become absorbed in taking care of children and seriously neglect both their responsibilities as a husband or wife and their own personal needs. Another example is the adult who becomes overextended in caring for a relative or friend who is disabled or terminally ill. Sometimes heavy involvement in cases of this nature is called for, especially for short periods of time, but there are situations in which the extent of the activity is unnecessary or unwise. In addition, there is the example of young adults who are over involved with their parents. They have not developed the capacity to function on their own and to live their own lives. Consequently, they are constantly seeking their parents' approval and usually want to be with them on a continuous basis.

Moreover, a general unhealthy involvement with family, relatives, and friends is possible in which one to a large extent becomes absorbed in these immediate relationships. Undoubtedly most of us depend a great deal upon this immediate environment, because it provides us with our close associations and offers us acceptance and security. However, this context should not be our only source of identity and sense of obligation. Involve-

ment in family environment becomes extreme when responsibilities outside it are ignored. When this occurs, little or no effort is made to help
overcome social weaknesses or world problems, unless they in some way
affect what is close at hand. There is only a feeling of obligation to correct
what pertains to one's own area of life. At the same time, this perspective
does not necessarily imply a complete insensitivity to the misfortune of
those outside one's own sphere. It is possible for those with this outlook to
have some sense of concern for those in other environments. Yet, their
actions are held back by a limited vision of their own obligations. They see
their responsibilities as being for the most part restricted to the people that
they know and that live nearby.

DETACHMENT FROM SOCIETY

   Thus, in responding to the decisions concerning detachment and involvement, unhealthy acts of involvement are indeed possible, and there
are a variety of ways that they may occur. Nevertheless, the unhealthy
expressions in this regard especially common in recent years are centered
more in an overemphasis upon detachment. There has been an overall
social tendency in the last several decades toward becoming too isolated
from others. Even many of the situations of unhealthy involvement can also
be understood in terms of detachment. That is, they imply or often lead to
separation from others. For instance, overwork usually includes a considerable degree of estrangement from one's family, relatives, and friends, and a
preoccupation with one's immediate environment indicates that the person
is disengaged from the larger society and its problems.
   Even though there does seem to be a trend toward detachment, this does
not mean that Americans no longer value social relationships and closeness
with others. As Warren Johnson indicates, most people on the surface at
least still support the idea of community involvement. On a more fundamental level we have problems with it. We are attracted to neighborliness
and social interaction, but we do not like them when they restrict our
individual freedoms. We want to carry out our own activities whenever we
wish. It is not that we dislike community and social involvement; it is rather
that we prefer to maintain our sense of personal freedom.[4]
   These individual freedoms are strongly valued in our society, and one of
these is the freedom to live where we choose. This is a freedom that has
contributed to openness in our society and to many social changes, but at
the same time it has made it easier for individuals to detach themselves
from community involvement. Because of the option to move, it is possible
for people to exploit an area and neglect their social responsibilities. People

can simply move if there are problems in the community or if others are pressuring them to take some particular step toward improvement. As Johnson says,

> The freedom to move is an incentive for individuals to be irresponsible—to vote for low taxes, to skimp on public services, to cut corners on maintaining streets and public buildings, or to exploit the environment for economic gain—and then, before the results begin to show too obviously, to sell their property and move on.[5]

This pattern of behavior has been common in American history. Early settlers used the farm lands and forests until they were barren and depleted, and then they would move on to new areas. In this century Americans have deserted various locations in order to avoid problems of pollution, high crime levels, inferior education, and racial integration. The past several decades have witnessed the flight from the inner cities to the suburbs in order to achieve more pleasant living conditions. Also, many Americans have moved in recent years in an effort to escape contact with minority groups and to provide opportunities for their children to attend better schools.

People exercise their right to move as a way of dealing with or avoiding social problems. Instead of involving themselves in the community and seeking to improve the conditions, they relocate. In addition, there is an adjoining circumstance to this one which also encourages detachment. It concerns a type of mind-set that has become characteristic of many Americans in the last few decades. With the development of our mobile society, many people have acquired what can be called an attitude of mobility and assume they will soon be moving. When they move into an area, they regard it as temporary, and, consequently, they do not pursue any long-term relationships. Because they do not believe they will be staying long, they see no need to get involved in the community and its problems. Even when they remain in a given location for a long time, they continue to think they may move at any time. As a result, they stay detached from close interactions with others and from contributing to community projects.

Thus, there have been Americans who have isolated themselves from community activities by exercising their freedom to move to other areas and by developing an outlook of mobility. This seems to indicate an inclination within the American spirit toward avoiding social involvement. Philip Slater insists that Americans have definitely suffered from this tendency, and he points out numerous ways that this has been expressed. One way is in relation to the mass media. We sometimes use television, radio, magazines, and newspapers to escape any in-depth involvement in the issues. We like to think that this interaction with the mass media is a sufficient involvement in itself. Through the show or the article we convince ourselves that we have dealt with the problem. As Slater says,

> The TV documentary presents a tidy package with opposing news and an insinuation of progress. Printed articles and reviews give just the blend of titillation and condescension to make readers imagine that they're already "in" and need not undergo the experience itself—that they've not only participated in the novel adventure but already outgrown it. Thus the ultimate effect of the media is to reinforce the avoiding response by providing people with an effigy of confrontation.[6]

This avoiding tendency is also manifested by the fact that Americans are often overoptimistic about the solution to such problems as poverty, crime, unemployment, the energy crisis, and environmental pollution. We seek to escape becoming thoroughly involved in these problems by pretending that they have easy answers.[7] For instance, we like to think that science and technology will eventually give us a complete and safe solution to environmental pollution and that the energy crisis can be overcome if we could just keep the oil companies from exploiting the market. We also like to assume that crime could be eliminated, or at least substantially reduced, if we simply adopt stricter penalties for criminals. The quick acceptance of easy answers such as these keeps us from having to struggle with the complexity of the issues and from having to make personal sacrifices.

This inclination toward avoiding social involvement is further revealed in our emphasis on planning and superficial deeds at the expense of serious activities. It is not unusual for Americans to set up a procedure for dealing with a problem and even be willing to work on the beginning steps but be lax in carrying it through to completion. We want to think that all that is necessary to solve problems is to establish a committee, make a study, or write a report. Most of the time we do not want to put forth the effort or make the changes required to correct the problem.[8]

Another way that this avoiding tendency occurs is by means of what Slater calls the Toilet Assumption. This is a phenomenon that has grown out of some fairly recent changes in American society. It is now the case that many of the unsightly and unpleasant aspects of life are removed from our immediate experience. Human excretion is not present in the outhouse but is flushed down a toilet. Garbage does not remain nearby but disappears down a disposal unit or is carried off to another area. In order to eat meat at a meal, we no longer have to kill an animal or see it being killed nearby. Similarly, persons who are retarded, mentally ill, extremely old, severely sick, or dying usually are placed in institutions and are no longer a part of our everyday lives.[9]

No doubt positive qualities have resulted from these changes such as improved sanitation, increased personal convenience, and often a higher level of mental and physical care for various groups of the population. But it is also true, as Slayter says, that changes of this kind have made it more difficult to have a realistic view of life and have led to what he calls the Toilet Assumption. This is the notion that we like to pretend certain aspects of life do not exist when they no longer can be seen. It is the old principle of out of sight, out of mind, and it is definitely operative in the way that Americans relate to social problems.[10]

There are many possible instances today of the Toilet Assumption as it pertains to social issues. We may like to assume that such activities as illegal drugs and prostitution are not part of our city if they are not apparent in our neighborhood. Another possible assumption is that pollution is not especially threatening to American society because there are not any evident signs of it in the immediate vicinity. Also, since low income families often live in a separate section of the city, it is easy for someone to deny that poverty or unemployment exists in the area. In addition, the segregation of minority groups in our society such as blacks, Indians, and Mexicans has often made it difficult to recognize their problems.

DETACHMENT FROM CLOSE ASSOCIATIONS

The overall trend in American society in the last several decades has been in the direction of excessive detachment. So far the discussion has been primarily concerned with a general kind of disengagement from society and its problems. Does this trend also apply to what are usually considered the close associations of an individual? Does it apply to family members, relatives, neighbors, and friends? In response to this question, it does appear that these areas must also be included. There does seem to be a growing tendency in recent years toward greater isolation not only from society in general but also in our more immediate relationships. Many patterns of behavior are now present in which family ties are not as strong, friends and relatives do not have as much contact, and neighbors are more distant in their communications with each other.

A number of social developments are worth noting that have served to influence people toward this greater degree of detachment from family, relatives, friends, and neighbors. Increased wealth that our society has experienced has enabled us to purchase a larger number of mechanical devices for our use including radios, televisions, computers, stereos, and tape players. On the one hand, these instruments have given us pleasure and diversion and in some cases have disseminated information and provided learning opportunities. On the other hand, they have sometimes prevented people from having closer relationships with those around them. Instead of making an effort to interact with a friend or family member, it is often easier just to turn on a machine. To a great extent these devices allow us to have passive relationships without expending a great deal of energy. They also afford us the chance to exercise our own choices and for the most part do not restrict our interests and desires. Some people even become absorbed in these instruments and spend many hours each day attached to them. In the past there was a great deal of talk about people being addicted to watching television, and no doubt there are still many Americans who belong in this category. But now a mechanical addiction often mentioned is an obsession with the computer. Some people are so fascinated with these machines that they leave very little time for human interaction.

Our affluence has also made it possible for us to acquire many more personal possessions than in the past. There are many things that now are no longer held in common with others, but instead they are used or owned individually. Many of us, for instance, now have our own personal bed-rooms, bathrooms, and beds as well as our own radios, televisions, and telephones. This is typically considered to be a positive development in our culture, and obviously it is beneficial by supplying greater convenience, privacy, and comfort. At the same time it also carries with it certain drawbacks, at least in regard to human relationships. People are not forced as often to interact and share with each other, and, therefore, it is easier for individuals to go their own way and for alienation to set in. Furthermore, in the past an important means within the family by which children learned how to share with others was through common possessions. Consequently, this change undoubtedly makes it more difficult for people to acquire the ability to share and to acknowledge its value.

Another development that has encouraged detachment from close asso-ciations has been the increased rate of divorce and separation, which brings about changes in the life-style and relationships of those concerned. They must make adjustments to losing the companionship of a spouse, and if they have children, they must offer them an explanation and deal with their responses. Also, there is the problem of moving to another location which may result in the interruption of relationships with friends and relatives. In addition, there is the possibility that communication with friends and relatives will be hindered by a negative reaction to the situation on their part.

However, usually other people besides the couple are affected by their divorce or separation. Relatives and friends must adapt to the new circum-stances, especially the children. When children are present, their lives may be seriously disturbed by their parents' actions. They may react with anger or blame toward one or both of their parents, and it may be difficult for their parents to deal constructively with these feelings because of their own emotional stress. The social environment of children may also change in that they may have to move to another location or have lengthy visits away from home with one of their parents. Additionally, there are other possible problems for these children such as the rejection of friends or neighbors and limited opportunities for seeing relatives such as grandparents.

A third development has been the large increase in the number of women who work outside the home. Many benefits grow out of this practice including a higher standard of living for many families, more contributions to society from women, and greater opportunities for women to follow their interests and find self-fulfillment. However, this development can foster isolation and separation from family members, relatives, and friends. It is sometimes argued that a woman working outside the home does not necessarily neglect her responsibilities to her children, because it is the quality of time spent with children which is important and not the quantity of time. Certainly there is a great deal of truth in this argument. That which is important is the time that is productive toward the growth and enrichment of the child, and there is a sense in which it is usually possible for parents who both work to provide this for their children. The problem is that a quality of time implies the need for some quantity, and when the parents both work, it is extremely difficult to give an adequate amount of time to their children, in spite of good intentions. Along with responsibilities to children, so many other responsibilities demand one's time such as additional work requirements, duties around the house, personal responsibilities, and obligations to the church and community. Of course, it is not simply demands on one's time, but also there are limits to one's energy. When parents are especially tired, such as late in the evening after a day's work, it becomes exceedingly hard for them to make the effort required to have close interaction with their children.

Therefore, the frequent occurrence of both parents working has served to contribute to the growth of detachment between parents and children. Certainly this is not true in every case in which both parents work, but no doubt there are many families in which it is a factor. In fact, in some family situations the children are seriously neglected.

Moreover, it has not been unusual for the rise in the number of women working to stimulate detachment from friends and relatives. The limitations of time and energy have also made it more difficult for families to reach out to those outside the home. In the past when only a small percentage of women were working outside the home, it was often the woman of the family who initiated close relationships with friends and relatives. She talked with her neighbors, spent time with her friends, and invited friends and relatives for meals and visits. She often served as the instigator for the family of social events and external relationships. When the woman is working outside the home, it is much more difficult for her to carry out this role, and so often today she either does not do so or is less effective.

A further development that has led to this greater detachment in our more immediate relationships has been the increase in cynicism and distrust toward other people. There is now more widespread acceptance of the idea that people are just looking out for their own welfare and basically are not trustworthy. This attitude has been brought about by many different occurrences especially the larger number of divorces and separations. Not only have some divorces and separations given rise to this outlook on the part of the couple, but also some have affected children, relatives, and friends. Another factor that has promoted cynicism and distrust has been the growth of special interest groups and the attention given to their activities by the mass media. Protests, marches, strikes, and negotiations for higher wages and better working conditions are common practices in our society and are often reported by the newspaper, radio, and television. Still other situations encouraging skepticism include national events such as the Watergate crisis and the Iran-Contra scandal along with the presence of deceptive practices in politics, religion, business, and advertising. Therefore, a variety of circumstances has helped to foster increased cynicism and distrust in our society, and, consequently, some people have become more aloof and hesitant in their approach to others. They are less willing to disclose themselves and to establish intimate relationships.

A final development contributing to this detachment from our close associations has been the increase in geographical mobility. This was previously discussed in reference to detachment from society, but it should also be recognized that it effects this area as well. With frequent moving, it becomes difficult to have friends and maintain contact with relatives. As already indicated, constant moving also tends to create a perspective in which a person doesn't attempt to establish long-term relationships.

Several developments in our society, therefore, have helped bring about detachment from our family members, relatives, friends, and neighbors. Philip Zimbardo gives particular attention to our detachment from relatives and emphasizes that our relationships with them have been especially weakened in recent years by several factors. These include not only our mobility and the higher rate of divorce and separation but also the fact that many people have fewer relatives. The movement to smaller families means fewer sisters, brothers, aunts, uncles, cousins, nieces, and nephews than there were in the past. Zimbardo describes the demise of our relationships with relatives in the following way:

With relatives thousands of miles apart, ritual gatherings become rarer, and relatives become curious aliens to our children. The zero population growth movement has as one of its unintended consequences children with fewer siblings or cousins and eventually with few aunts or uncles. The paucity of relatives, coupled with the fact of delayed childbearing and the high divorce rate, mean there will be fewer of us with a sense of primal ties to many kin and of roots that run deep into one place, our "home."[11]

AN IMPROVED PERSPECTIVE TOWARD DETACHMENT AND INVOLVEMENT

Hence, the two main areas in which conflicts between detachment and involvement arise are decisions concerning society in general and those about one's close associations. As people seek to answer the variety of questions growing out of these areas, they tend to develop their own way of viewing these conflicts along with certain patterns of behavior in responding to them. Sometimes these habitual ways of behaving are unhealthy, and in recent years these unhealthy expressions have more commonly taken the form of excessive detachment.

What can be said about an improved way of dealing with these conflicts between detachment and involvement? What constitutes the right approach toward these conflicts, which in turn would make possible healthy patterns of behavior? One thing that can be said about the proper approach is that it includes an appreciation of both detachment and involvement. It recognizes that both are necessary for the well-being of the individual as well as others. There are times when isolation from relationships is required and other times when involvement is called for. It is also understood that there are occasions when one may have to withdraw from a particular type of involvement activity in order to make room for another. That is, in some situations one kind of involvement may take priority over another, even though both may be considered to some degree worthy. Examples include the person who on a given occasion chooses to be with family members instead of friends and the individual who on a particular evening takes time to work on a social project instead of visiting with relatives.

Improved perspective toward detachment and involvement also has a broad understanding of these concepts. There is the acknowledgment of a large range of responsibilities that flow out of both detachment and involvement. Consequently, a narrow preoccupation with only a few responsibilities is avoided. For instance, in regard to detachment there is the affirmation of the need not only for passive acts such as studying and reflection but also more active endeavors such as recreation and bodily exercise. In the realm of involvement there is not merely an allegiance, for example, to those people that one knows well and that live nearby, but there is also an acceptance of responsibilities toward those who belong to different social groups from one's own.

Even though this approach adopts a variety of responsibilities from the concepts of detachment and involvement, this does not mean that these obligations should all be given equal emphasis. Undoubtedly some responsibilities should generally take priority over others. For instance, if one has the opportunity to meet the genuine needs of a friend, these should usually be given priority over certain personal obligations such as sleep, proper diet, and physical exercise. It should be recognized that certain circumstances arise where responsibility may have to be seriously neglected in order to meet the pressing needs at the time. One example would be that people may not be able to meet their vocational, social, and personal obligations adequately if a family member, relative, or friend is severely ill. Another example is when vocational and social duties demand a period of time requiring family responsibilities to be neglected. Yet, a proper approach to detachment and involvement will certainly attempt to achieve a balance in every area of responsibility and will seek to avoid the neglect of a given area for long periods of time. When possible, this approach will also try to compensate for a previously neglected area by giving it more time and attention in the future.

Furthermore, this approach has a high level of awareness of the present trend in our society toward excessive detachment. There especially is an alertness to the fact that this social tendency can easily infringe upon one's own life. It is easy for socially acceptable and popular activities simply to be adopted and carried out without giving full consideration to all of their possible consequences for oneself and the lives of others. When something receives the stamp of approval of the American life-style, then it becomes hard to resist and even difficult to think about objectively. Social pressure is exerted to conform and to assume a cause is justifiable. Many socially approved activities currently encourage detachment including extensive television watching, frequent moving from one place to another, long hours of work, both parents working outside the home, and the institutionalization of the elderly. This is not to say that activities such as these are wrong and should always be avoided, for often they may be necessary. It is to say that they should be thoroughly examined before they are undertaken or encouraged. The right kind of perspective makes conscious and thoughtful decisions about these activities and definitely gives careful attention to how they might affect human relationships.

Moreover, this perspective is willing to make the effort that is required to have the proper kind of involvement with others. As Philip Zimbardo emphasizes, we must think more in terms of people being our most cherished resource and be willing to work hard to maintain our close relationships with others.[12] An individual must go beyond simply concentrating upon personal goals and concerns and give more attention to the lives of others. An active interest should be taken in neighbors and relatives and in those who live in other parts of society and in other countries. This also demands that a strong sense of organization and self-discipline be developed in a person's daily life-style. Consequently, more time is available for involvement activities and it will be more likely that responsibilities will be carried out even when they are not immediately pleasurable.

NOTES

1. Wayne E. Oates, *Confessions of a Workaholic* (Nashville: Abingdon, 1971) 3.
2. Ibid., 3–7.
3. Ibid., 9–21, 113–14.
4. Warren Johnson, *The Future Is Not What it Used to Be* (New York: Dodd, Mead and Company, 1985) 140–42.
5. Ibid., 140–41.
6. Philip Slater, *The Pursuit of Loneliness* (Boston: Beacon Press, 1976) 23.
7. Ibid., 18–20.
8. Ibid., 20–21.
9. Ibid., 21–23.
10. Ibid.
11. Philip G. Zimbardo, "The Age of Indifference," *Psychology Today*, 14 (August, 1980) 76.
12. Ibid.

DISCUSSION QUESTIONS

1. What are some specific ways that a person might contribute to the betterment of society and assist in overcoming its problems?

2. Are there some ways in which our society encourages people toward overwork? If so, what are the ones you would mention?

3. What are the various obligations to oneself that are referred to within the chapter? Are there others that you are aware of?

4. What are the moral obligations of an individual who is asking someone to volunteer for an activity or perform a task? Does this individual have a responsibility to help the other person avoid becoming overextended?

5. Do you think the attitude of mobility affects a large number of people in our society? Is it possible for it to affect college students in relationship to their college environment?

6. What are examples of overoptimistic and easy answers that are sometimes set forth as solutions for the complex problems of our society?

7. What is the Toilet Assumption and what particular examples of it are given within the chapter? What additional examples are you able to mention?

8. Do you think parents should restrict their children in terms of the quantity and quality of television viewing that is allowed? Do you think they should also restrict themselves in this regard?

9. Do you think that for their own welfare some people require more periods of isolation from outward relationships than others? Do you think some people require more extensive involvement in outward activities than others?

10. Is one's responsibility in providing aid for a friend usually greater than the responsibility to provide it for an acquaintance or stranger?

CASE STUDIES

1. Joan Anderson has a large family and has recently had to go to work to supplement her husband's income. For a long time she has been active in her church, but she decided to restrict her church involvement in order to carry out her responsibilities to her family. Now she is being asked to assume many of the old activities in the church. She knows that she does not have the time and would have to neglect her family if she accepted these duties. However, she feels that she has an obligation to her church. She also has experienced social rejection by several persons in the church because she has not been heavily involved. She is a sensitive person and would like to avoid this rejection. What should she do?

2. Bill Milton is married with three small children and is heavily involved in community activities. He teaches a Sunday School class at his church and is chairman of a church committee. He also is an officer in a civic club and does volunteer work for a group that helps low income families in the area. The problem that he faces is that his community involvement along with the work he has to do at night for his job leave him few opportunities for other activities. He is not able to spend much time with his family and is unable to find time for recreation and physical exercise. Bill is trying to decide whether or not he should continue with his present life-style or perhaps make some changes. Do you think he should make some changes? If so, what specifically would you suggest?

3. Brad and Susan Wilson are considering the possibility of moving to a city that is about one thousand miles from where they currently live. They are both interested in the jobs available in the new location and think they would like them better than the jobs they now have. Susan's new job would have a similar income to her present one, but Brad would have one that carries with it a much larger salary. The Wilsons have three children, ages twelve, fourteen, and sixteen, and the additional income would especially be helpful in financing their education. However, Brad and Susan are aware that their family has been happy where they now live and that the children are strongly opposed to moving. The children have their close friends that they don't want to leave, and also they enjoy the company of relatives that live in the area. The children have two sets of grandparents as well as several uncles, aunts, and cousins that live within a hundred mile radius of their home. Do you think the Wilsons should move? Why?

SUGGESTIONS FOR FURTHER READING

Bohannan, Paul. *All the Happy Families: Exploring the Varieties of Family Life.* New York: McGraw-Hill Book Company, 1985.

Clecak, Peter. *America's Quest for the Ideal Self.* New York: Oxford University Press, 1983.

Fawcett, Edmund and Thomas, Tony. *The American Condition.* New York: Harper and Row, 1982.

Johnson, Warren. *The Future Is Not What it Used to Be.* New York: Dodd, Mead and Company, 1985.

Oates, Wayne E. *Confessions of a Workaholic.* Nashville: Abingdon, 1971.

Slater, Philip. *The Pursuit of Loneliness.* Boston: Beacon Press, 1976.

CHAPTER 5
INDEPENDENCE AND DEPENDENCE

A final conflict which overlaps somewhat with detachment and involvement may be referred to by the categories of independence and dependence. It is true that the various forms of involvement often indicate the carrying out of acts of dependence and that expressions of detachment are frequently accompanied by autonomous responses. However, it is also the case that involvement may utilize autonomous behavior and that detachment may include dependent actions. This indicates that these two conflicts are different with distinctive questions and concepts arising in each. Whereas the controversy surrounding detachment and involvement concerns whether or not to extend oneself in outward relationships, the issue of independence and dependence asks if one should rely upon others or oneself.

The discussion in this chapter points out a paradox that exists between independence and dependence. At the same time that we have a need for autonomy we also are living in a state of dependence. This chapter explores the meaning of this paradox as it occurs in various areas of life and insists that in our everyday decisions we should strive to maintain a balance between independence and dependence.

THE STRUGGLE FOR AUTONOMY

Autonomy is the will to think and act for oneself. It is the ability to make one's own decisions and direct one's own actions. Those who respond autonomously are able to govern their own lives instead of being dominated by the expectations of parents, the interests of friends, or the influences of society. They do not necessarily become isolated from others and simply function alone, although unfortunately that is sometimes the case. In a healthy form of autonomy people continue to interact with others, maintain intimate relationships, and experience belonging to a group. They stay in contact with others and still make decisions for themselves about their values, goals, and behavior.

The struggle to attain autonomy starts at an early age. Erik Erikson says it arises as a conflict as early as age two or three when, for instance, children begin to realize that they have the power to cling to parents or push them away.[1] Even though this struggle begins in the first few years of life, this does not mean that it can eventually be overcome, for the struggle continues throughout life without ever completely subsiding. There is always a conflict between deciding for oneself and letting others have control. Indeed, there are periods of time when the struggle is especially intense such as during young adulthood when questions arise about life-style, vocation, and marriage. At these points in life an individual may make critical movements either toward or away from autonomy. However, even when a person becomes decisively more autonomous than in the past, the struggle is not over. Decisions have to be made continually, and it is possible at any one time for an individual to regress to a point of weaker autonomy.

One way of perceiving the quest for autonomy is in outward terms of struggle with others to attain the self that one needs to be. In this case the search is a movement away from conformity, doing what is expected, pleasing others, and constantly seeking to be liked. Simultaneously it is a movement toward self-direction, independent thinking, personal integrity, and freedom to be oneself. Everyone constantly comes in contact with the desires and expectations of others, and there are always individuals who encourage us in certain directions along with aspects of society which influence us. Efforts of others may simply be intended as a means of manipulation and control, but this is not always the case. Sometimes they result from basically good motives in that persons such as parents and friends may sincerely be thinking of our welfare. Regardless of the circumstances, autonomy demands that we evaluate ideas for ourselves and make our own decisions. It requires that when necessary we have the courage to disagree and be different.

Gordon Allport portrays this struggle as being one between tribalism and individuation which he says are two forces serving as a basis of conflict throughout our lives. The tribe represents the pull upon us of the family and community. From the beginning of life it provides us with love and security along with our early standards of conduct and definitions of the world around us, but at the same time it is also the force that leads us toward conformity and conventional conduct. However, another force counteracts the tribe and urges the person toward self-assertion. Even in childhood this force calls upon the person to resist what can be the smothering effects of the social environment. It antagonizes the individual as if it realizes that tribal demands can be a threat to one's personal integrity.[2]

Wayne Oates speaks of autonomy as being freedom from pack thinking. He describes this type of thinking as being characterized by crowd pleasing, propaganda, partyline cliches, and the bandwagon approach, and he points out that it would be relatively easy to resist if it were not for the necessity of community. We need the approval of others and fellowship with others, and this tends to pull us in the direction of pack thinking. However, he warns that we also have a need for personal integrity and to exercise our individuality through independent judgments, which must be balanced against our desire for community. He further warns that those who seek to rid themselves of pack thinking and to take a stand for justice and reconciliation had better be ready for opposition from others. Those who do not take sides are often despised by those who do.[3]

Oates tells of how he struggled with pack thinking in his own role as a Christian minister. He soon realized as a young pastor he was expected to give priority to the church as an institution. He was supposed to get people to come to church and try to convert them to Christianity. This meant that he had to put forth a certain image and learn the right words and phrases to say. At first he tried hard to conform to this pattern, but soon he recognized that this approach was not adequate. He began to resist pack thinking by seeking to minister to every aspect of the person and by emphasizing a growth oriented perspective. He also sought to take an interest in all of the people around him regardless of whether they attended church. He cites several experiences in which he was able to help certain people who were largely ignored by the rest of the community.[4] Oates insists that

> Pack thinking about the Christian witness focuses on the church as an institution that people serve. Salvation becomes a package of right words and phrases to say. The pastor is taught, prompted, urged, and paid to "traverse sea and land" to make proselytes (Matthew 23:15). I have no inhibition in forthrightly proclaiming the good news of God in Jesus Christ for the redemption of persons. However, I turn again and again to Jesus' own manner of resisting the package thinking of his day and pinpointing the good news of the Kingdom at the site of peoples' most personal fears, burdens, complex relationships, illnesses, and loneliness.[5]

Autonomy, therefore, is an outward struggle with conformity and the expectations of others, and also it is an inward struggle with oneself. Erikson speaks of the conflict between autonomy and a person's sense of shame and self-doubt. When there is a loss of independent thinking and control of one's own actions, then a person begins to be dominated by shame and doubt producing a general feeling of inadequacy and an inability to be oneself. Erikson emphasizes that people begin to experience this conflict at a young age and that it is important that children develop an early trust in themselves. They must not feel that they are always in jeopardy when they make their own choices and express themselves. If they are constantly rejected or punished for their efforts at self-sufficiency, then strong feelings of shame and doubt are the result.[6]

Also, experiences of anxiety offer opposition to autonomy. Anxiety is a disturbing feeling within that accompanies the risk and uncertainty involved in personal freedom and autonomous decision making. It is analogous to fear, but it does not have a specific object or circumstance which calls it forth. However, it can be quite intense and can serve to drive an individual away from exercising autonomy. Rollo May points out that anxiety can be either constructive or destructive depending on the response of the individual. On the one hand, it may arouse us and force us to use our imagination and to think. In this way it may stimulate us toward creative ideas and acts of discovery. On the other hand, it may paralyze us and isolate us and lead us toward withdrawal or conformity.[7]

May also speaks of the relationship between anxiety and what he calls pauses in our lives. A pause is an unfilled time period when we are open to what is possible and new. It offers us the opportunity to reflect, wonder, create, and have a sense of awe. Also, a pause is the moment in which a person is most vulnerable to anxiety. Consequently, many people flee from pauses by filling them with whatever is available. They may always have the company of a television or radio, or they may try to make their schedules as busy as possible. However, in avoiding pauses in their lives, people tend to limit their autonomy and sacrifice many of their chances for enrichment and growth.[8]

Hence, there is a basic need for autonomy within the self, and each person struggles throughout life in an effort to achieve it. Even though emphasis thus far has been upon this sense of autonomy, it must also be remembered that dependence is a significant aspect of human existence. Human nature is such that we rely upon much outside ourselves for fulfillment, meaning, and life itself. We depend upon other human beings in a number of ways including the care and nurture of parents, the love and companionship of friends and relatives, and the assistance from the knowledge and skills of others in society. We further rely upon other forms of life and nonliving substances for some of the essential ingredients of life such as food, water, air, heat, shelter, and clothing. Many also feel an important sense in which we are dependent upon the Divine and that God created us and sustains our existence, and a relationship with him provides acceptance, strength, guidance, contentment, love, and hope.

A paradox, therefore, exists in human existence. While we are struggling for a sense of autonomy, we are also living in a state of dependence. As we make our own decisions we must recognize our various forms of dependence. We need autonomy, but we also need to acknowledge and accept our sense of dependence.

THE PARADOX IN THE SELECTION OF IDEAS

Many areas of life create this paradox and present questions of independence and dependence. One of these concerns the selection of ideas to be followed. No doubt everyone depends upon others in some manner for knowledge about life and events in the world. We rely upon others for information that is predominantly factual such as news reporting, basic educational instruction, and the everyday description of events, but there are also numerous occasions when we utilize advice from others that includes a significant degree of judgment and assessment on their part. This advice may pertain to the broader questions of one's major values, religious beliefs, and general life-style. More often it is related to ordinary situations and problems that people typically experience. That is, it is not unusual for others to offer us suggestions about such matters as the meaning of a current event, the competence of a certain medical doctor, the reliability of a particular product, or the worthiness of some upcoming community activity.

However, even though there are times when each person practices some degree of dependence upon the ideas of others, there are still questions that arise at this point. One concerns when information should be sought. Often we gain knowledge or receive advice without seeking it, but at other times it is not available to us unless we ask for it or make an effort to acquire it. Examples would be the student who must decide whether to ask for clarification about a complex concept presented in the textbook or the person who must make a decision about getting advice about a personal illness or physical abnormality.

When it is determined that assistance should be sought, another question that must be addressed is in regard to the source to be used. Who or what will serve as the means for acquiring the information? A student, for instance, may pursue an explanation for an unclear concept in a variety of ways such as by asking the professor, talking to a classmate, or by doing additional reading. Occasionally, a single source may be enough to consult, if it provides accurate information. A person may contact the wrong source which may furnish erroneous or incomplete information. For example, a person with a physical illness may be misled by the advice of a friend, or a person inquiring about a political candidate may be misinformed by prejudicial statements. Even though it is possible for a single source to be sufficient, it is often advantageous to contact several sources to encounter divergent viewpoints and to offer a greater opportunity to gain more widespread information and perspectives. Multiple sources are especially beneficial in regard to issues that are controversial and value laden. So often our thinking is limited or even distorted because we refer to only one source or one kind of source. For instance, we might only listen to what our friends or relatives are saying about a social problem, or we might simply study a religious issue from one particular outlook.

A further question refers to how the sources are received. Truth is more readily acquired when a sincere and honest effort is made to determine what others intend by their statements and then their ideas are carefully examined and evaluated. Unfortunately a person may have adopted perspectives which interfere with this process so that limited understandings and false ideas are affirmed. One such barrier to the proper reception of sources is the presence of prejudices. These are preconceived viewpoints which are grounded in judgments made before the evidence is adequately considered. As the term itself indicates, they are prejudgments, or in other words, judgments made before one is really prepared to make them. They are usually negative in that they set forth an unfavorable response or some type of opposition to something such as those expressed against members of certain races, minorities, religions, countries, and vocations. However, prejudices may also express favorable attitudes. These are often accompanied by a naive or unrealistic attitude as is sometimes present in prejudices toward country, home town, or alma mater.

Frequently prejudices originate in childhood or youth so that by adulthood many prejudices have been present for years. Also, in some cases prejudices are a means by which people deal with various fears and anxieties and acquire personal security, and in other cases they serve as a basis for achieving social identity and group belonging. It is common for prejudices to carry strong emotions with them and to be firmly set within the individual. As a result, one's own prejudices are usually difficult to recognize, and when they are acknowledged, they may be even more of a problem to overcome.

Another misleading approach to the sources of ideas is authoritarianism. No doubt authorities can be a beneficial means of gaining information, as may be true in regard to educational programs, medical assessments, and news reports. But authoritarianism takes the use of authorities too far in the sense that certain individuals or groups are perceived in a blind and uncritical manner and are simply assumed to always be correct. Information is thought to be true just because it comes from a particular source such as a relative, friend, or leader in the community. Their ideas are affirmed without being considered and evaluated, and little effort is made to consult other sources. The problem is especially apparent when authorities enunciate ideas outside their field of expertise. People who practice authoritarianism usually will accept uncritically what their source says regardless of what area of life is being discussed.

Three areas in our society particularly vulnerable to the use of authoritarianism are politics, religion, and advertising. It is not unusual for political and religious leaders to be chosen and followed primarily on the basis of their personality and charisma; consequently, little or no attention is given to analyzing and determining the merit of their ideas. In the field of advertising, it is a common practice for movie stars, sports heroes, and famous Americans to be used for promoting various messages and products. In these presentations attempts at gaining support are made by focusing upon the emotional appeal of the individual instead of providing genuine evidence for what is being set forth.

THE PARADOX IN PERSONAL RELATIONSHIPS

Thus, choices about ideas to be followed often contain the paradox of independence and dependence so that questions arise about when and how one should depend upon the ideas of others. This paradox also is present in our relationships with other people. Many relationships are casual ones which revolve around the production and interchange of goods and services. Of course, we live in a highly specialized and interrelated society where an individual usually works solely in one particular occupation in a single segment of the economy. Each worker concentrates on a certain task resulting in society having an interdependent structure. Most of what a person needs and uses in everyday life comes from the efforts of other people. For example, most people do not grow their own food, build their own houses, or make their clothing, implements, or machines. Also, we do not rely primarily upon ourselves for our educational, medical, and legal concerns. Instead, in each case we frequently turn to others for assistance, and on many occasions we depend heavily upon the skills of others.

A question occurs concerning the individual response made to this state of social dependence existing in America. Because of the interdependent character of our society, a large number of us have never learned to perform many of the basic tasks of life. Therefore, many would find it quite difficult, to say the least, to have to live under circumstances without the help of others. As a result of this dependence, it might be thought that we would have an outlook of gratitude toward others and a strong sense of belonging and closeness to others. Certainly this can be the result when people carefully reflect on the situation and gain a realistic and authentic view of themselves and their country. However, gratitude unfortunately is not the typical response, and instead a great deal of irony exists in this facet of American life. Although we are extremely dependent upon others to help us meet life's demands and satisfy our desires, we often like to think of ourselves as being able to function entirely on our own. That is, it is common for Americans to be restricted by feelings of individualism and not fully recognize this sense of reliance upon other people. Consequently, the potential that these circumstances have for bringing about appreciation for others and community spirit usually never has the opportunity to develop in a person's life.

In addition to our dependence upon the skills of numerous people within the social structure, we also rely upon certain individuals for close interaction. Everyone needs certain persons who will accept us and share our interests and concerns. Each of us must have at least some close attachments to experience companionship, affection, confirmation, and security. One question at this point concerns who exactly will be included in these close relationships. These choices, of course, must be determined by the individuals involved, but a basic consideration is that associations must be mutual. Close relationships have a two-way character and are not effective unless both parties are interested enough to join with each other. Sometimes illegitimate methods are used in an effort to force these relationships to occur. However, these efforts often fail in the long run, because coercion, manipulation, and trickery do not usually produce a genuine sense of closeness. Furthermore, even though it is true that people may change or gradually develop these relationships, one should not expect each association, or even a large number of them, to become close. Generally only a small minority of the contacts that a person has ever turn out to be workable relationships.

Another question concerns how far one should go in close associations in being dependent upon others for acceptance and companionship. What balance should exist between independence and dependence in these relationships? It is indeed possible to become overly dependent upon someone to the point of failing in one's responsibilities in other interactions. One may get so caught up in intimacy with one individual that other relationships are largely ignored. This may happen within a family or between friends, but the classic example is the romantically involved couple who together block out the outside world and treat it with indifference. Also, people in this kind of intimacy sometimes lose or are unable to develop sufficient ability to function on their own. They may be unable to make their own decisions or act for themselves such as the man or woman who heavily relies upon a spouse for decision making and performing everyday tasks.

It is also possible for people to become overly independent in this area. That is, they find it difficult to maintain close relationships with others or are unable to enter them initially. Maxine Schnall indicates that in recent years many women in our society have especially had problems in this regard. She says that to a large extent women have been liberated from their traditional role, but often they have gone too far in the direction of independence. Many are determined to avoid the exploitation that pla-gued their mothers in marriage; consequently, they have suppressed their normal dependence needs as signs of weakness. Some have been exploited themselves in past relationships with the opposite sex and have feelings of resentment. Therefore, they prefer not to enter into any new relationships. Others are preoccupied with their own sense of freedom and do not want to risk losing it. They are afraid that any commitment on their part would mean entrapment.[9]

Therefore, a certain amount of both dependence and independence is necessary in close interactions in a person's life. On the one hand, each person's need for relationships should be acknowledged and accepted. An effort using legitimate methods is called for to initiate and maintain these relationships with compatible individuals. On the other hand, it must be remembered that one has other relationships and responsibilities besides these. An individual must avoid becoming captivated by intimate feelings to the point that there is no longer a broad sense of obligation toward others or an ability to think and act autonomously.

THE PARADOX IN THE WORKPLACE

The paradox of independence and dependence is a constant in our decisions about relationships with other people. This includes, moreover, relationships within the workplace in our society. There are many institu-tions with a variety of purposes such as business, educational, religious, governmental, or medical. Regardless of the type of organization where one is employed, certain personal relationships are typically experienced including interaction with fellow workers and supervisors. In addition, there is possible contact with people who are involved in the organization, but are not employed by it. They are the ones, the outside participants, who are offered the services and products of the institution such as customers, patients, clients, students, and laypersons.

On the one hand, there is a kind of dependence that prevails from the beginning of all work relationships. A person often needs the assistance and cooperation of fellow workers in order to carry out one's job properly and effectively. A person also depends upon superiors for instruction, leadership, encouragement, and just to remain employed in the organiza-tion. Furthermore, employees recognize dependence upon outside partici-pants because without them the work would not be necessary. They make a job necessary and give it purpose.

On the other hand, there are questions concerning the degree of depen-dence and the attitudes adopted. Some of these are decisions about relying upon coworkers for understanding job responsibilities and institutional perspectives. One may be aware that the views and attitudes of other workers are not adequate in instances of irresponsible work habits or acts which take unfair advantage of the organization. When the individual worker disagrees in such cases, then a decision has to be made about whether to act autonomously. One may recognize that certain superiors in the organization are inefficient or unethical in their work habits. As a result, a decision has to be made about whether to correct them or disagree with them. Independent behavior in this regard may on occasion jeopardize one's opportunities within the institution. Additional decisions must be made about the extent to which one relies upon outside participants for praise and acceptance. There may be circumstances in which these participants do not like or appreciate what genuinely contributes to their growth and well-being such as newspaper readers that demand editorials promoting their own philosophy, students who want merely to be entertained, and patients that always expect to be pampered and never corrected. Consequently, one has to determine whether to risk criticism or rejection in order to provide these persons with what is challenging and genuinely constructive.

Along with these considerations growing out of individual relationships, there also are questions of independence and dependence which pertain to the norms of the institution. Each of the vocations has a set of expectations that the member is supposed to follow, and the person must decide whether to adopt and rely upon them. Peter Berger points to some vocational norms when he speaks of the views expected of young people in different fields. He contrasts the philosophy expected of a young instructor in a university with what is expected from a young business school graduate. The young instructor, he says, must not have any political allegiance to the Republican party and must not talk in terms of the virtues of the corporation. This individual also must support the feminist movement and avoid expressing opposition to related issues. Conversely, the young person entering the business world is expected to affirm a conservative political stance. At the same time, this individual must not get involved in certain social efforts such as the environmental, antinuclear, or consumer movements.[10]

Of course, vocational norms do not simply concern one's philosophy. They also relate to other aspects of the work situation such as dress, personal conduct, and actual vocational practices. Whatever the nature of these vocational norms, decisions must be made about whether to conform to them. Undoubtedly a person must evaluate these norms and at times be willing to challenge them. This does not mean that all norms must be challenged but occasionally to be constructive, creative, or compassionate, certain norms must be opposed.

History furnishes many examples of persons who were willing to go against vocational norms. Socrates in ancient Greece dared to be different from the Sophists who were the professional teachers of the time. For instance, he refused to take money for his teaching, and this no doubt contributed to the dislike that many Sophists had for him. Jesus had the courage to be different from the religious teachers of his time. He, for instance, took his ministry to the outcasts of society, and the religious leaders criticized him for this. Religious leaders were not supposed to associate with tax collectors, the blind, and those in poverty. Another example of a person who was willing to oppose vocational norms was Martin Luther King, Jr. He was criticized for getting involved in social issues. Pastors are just not supposed to do that, at least not to the extent he did.

Let us look at norms within some of the different vocations today that need to be challenged for the good of both the vocations themselves and the rest of society. In the medical profession a norm resists changes in the health care system in our society and insists that any governmental intervention into the organization and distribution of medical services would necessarily be harmful. This norm must be questioned so that there can be more involvement by the medical profession in seeking to improve the system. Moreover, in the teaching profession there is the long-established norm that lecturing is the only method, or at least the superior method, to be used in teaching. This norm is currently being challenged but further opposition is needed. More attention needs to be given to the development of other methods of teaching. A further example is that some vocations have some fairly strong norms about the fees charged for services. Persons in these vocations are expected by other members not to charge less for these services. These norms ought to be questioned in order to give more freedom for the person to charge less or not to charge at all, at least under certain circumstances.

These are examples of vocational norms, expectations that are common to an entire vocation or at least a large majority of the institutions within a vocation. Along with these norms there are in addition what can be called institutional norms. These are expectations which characterize a particular institution but not necessarily all or a majority of the institutions within the vocation. Certainly it is the case that some of these norms also need to be challenged. For instance, in some institutions a form of discrimination may be a norm. In certain businesses, the employees may be expected to accept at least passively that members of minority groups are never promoted past a certain level, that women are not paid as much as men for the same job, and that employees must retire or accept a lower position once they reach their late 50s or early 60s. Furthermore, authoritarianism is a norm in many institutions. Workers are expected to carry out instructions in an unquestioning manner even if a bad decision or an unethical act is required. In hospitals, nurses may be expected to blindly implement the orders of a physician even though they may be based on false information or a misdiagnosis.

A BALANCE BETWEEN INDEPENDENCE AND DEPENDENCE

Hence, there is a paradox between independence and dependence which exists as we make decisions in many areas of life. We need autonomy, but we also have to recognize our state of dependence. Moreover, as we function in the midst of this paradox in everyday life, we must keep both of these needs in focus. That is, we must seek a balance between autonomy and dependence. We must strive to make decisions which help us to develop a healthy sense of autonomy but which also serve to maintain a proper form of dependence. How is this possible? What is it that contributes to the presence of this balance?

A number of qualities provide assistance in reaching the proper balance between independence and dependence. Courage is a significant one of these. Moral courage is often necessary in order to think and act for oneself and not be dominated by others. Many times courage is required for one to respond in a distinctive manner and to stand up for what is considered true or right. It is this kind of courage which enables a person to be authentic and act autonomously. However, moral courage must also be accompanied by what can be called social courage. Social courage allows a person to exercise a sense of dependence upon others. It is the courage that it takes to open oneself up to another human being in the hope of achieving a meaningful relationship. This involves courage because opening up to another person means that one becomes vulnerable to some extent. A person always risks being rejected or hurt.

The practice of courage implies the ability to overcome fear. Rollo May speaks of two types of fear that have to be confronted so that we may live courageous lives. One is the fear of being abandoned, the fear that others will not want to associate with us, and that we will be left all alone. This fear can be beneficial because it can encourage us to acknowledge our need for others and incline us toward personal interaction. If it is too strongly emphasized, it may have destructive consequences. It may result in relationships in which one's self is absorbed by others and loses its personal autonomy.[11]

The other kind of fear to be dealt with is the fear of losing one's self and being controlled by others. It is the fear of having one's independence taken away. It can constructively stimulate the protection of one's autonomy, but if it is given too much weight, it can also be harmful. It can lead to an individual being overly distrustful toward others and especially hesitant about entering into close relationships. In extreme cases it may lead to severe alienation and even social isolation.[12]

Other qualities which can contribute to the correct relationship between independence and dependence are certain forms of understanding and appreciation. With recognition of the part others play in one's life along with an attitude of gratitude, one has a greater potential for accepting the gifts that others have to offer. The development of a sense of appreciation implies more willingness to interact with others, gain from their abilities, and enter into close relationships. An individual must also have a sense of understanding and appreciation of oneself. The realization of one's own uniqueness and one's personal capacities and talents can give rise to healthy feelings of self-respect and self-confidence. With this appreciation of oneself, an individual has a stronger foundation for acting in an autonomous manner. There is the affirmation that one's thoughts and actions have worth and that one has the ability to contribute to society.

A further quality which assists in bringing about a proper balance between independence and dependence is a realistic approach toward both others and oneself. That is, there should not be expectations toward others and oneself that far exceed what is possible and normal. In regard to one's attitude toward others, one should not always expect others, even friends and relatives, to agree with and accept one's ideas and behavior. Also, one should understand that many other people have different personalities, interests, ideologies, values, and goals from our own. Consequently, not everyone will like us or appreciate us for who we are. In addition, our attitude toward ourselves must acknowledge that we may make mistakes or be unable to carry out what we intend. We may embarrass ourselves and may not always speak or act the way we wish we had. Thus, a sense of realism is important in being able to maintain a balance between independence and dependence. It helps us to continue to be autonomous and open toward others even when we face unfavorable responses or unpleasant and disappointing experiences.

Several characteristics, therefore, offer assistance in seeking a balance between independence and dependence. A question that arises at this point for religious faith concerns what this balance means in regard to one's relationship to God. Is the achievement of balance beneficial to this relationship? In response to this question, it should be noted that there is an important sense in which this balance is part of one's relationship with God. One's interaction with both others and oneself represents two dimensions of the Divine encounter and should not be rigidly separated in one's thinking from a faith response. Believers honor and show reverence to God by exercising the proper behavior toward his creation. In other words, one way of worshiping God is through the right kind of actions toward others and also the correct type of treatment of oneself. Acquiring a balance between independence and dependence must be seen as contributing to one's association with the Divine. It serves to strengthen these two dimensions of being in relationship to him.

However, this balance between independence and dependence obviously calls for an affirmation of the need for individual autonomy. How is this affirmation related to an overall need for dependence upon God? Is individual autonomy reconcilable with a need to rely upon the Divine? For believers, these two ideas can definitely be joined consistently, but there must be a constructive understanding of both of them. In regard to autonomy, it is certainly possible for it to take a form that is alien to any sort of faith in God in that it can simply be an effort to think and act on one's own without allowing for any reference to the Divine. In order for individual autonomy to be reconcilable with dependence upon God it must be viewed as existing in conjunction with faith; it is seen as a way of cooperating with the Divine. It is interpreted as a process that God uses in working with the individual to carry out Divine purposes. Moreover, perceiving autonomy as being in conjunction with faith further means that autonomy allows for the support of faith. The individual is willing to accept the guidance and strength which God provides for carrying out this activity.

What about dependence upon the Divine? What kind of understanding of this dependence is compatible with personal autonomy? It should first be pointed out that there are two different meanings of this notion. One concerns God's sustaining power over the universe and his ability to alter our lives. We depend upon God for life itself and for what he can help us to be. In this sense our dependence upon God simply exists in the nature of things and is not subject to choice. The other meaning of depending upon God is subject to our choice. In this sense to rely upon the Divine means that we accept him and make him part of our lives. We enter into a close relationship with him and utilize the personal gifts that he provides for us. That is, we recognize the need that we have for him in our lives and seek to relate to him.

It is especially this latter meaning of dependence which must be appropriately defined if dependence upon God and individual autonomy are to function together. It is certainly possible for this dependence to be understood in a manner which denies autonomy such as, for example, when emotionalism is practiced. Emotionalism in this area gives blind allegiance to one's immediate feelings and is highly skeptical of individual thinking. It assumes that these feelings always give us what God intends and that thinking activities are largely set apart from God's involvement in human affairs. However, if dependence upon God is to be reconciled with personal autonomy, the independent thinking process of the individual must to a great extent be sanctioned. This does not imply that the possibility of error in the process is denied, but it does mean that there is a general acknowledgment that autonomy has value in one's relationship to God. Many believe that God is frequently involved in this activity and often uses it to communicate his will.

NOTES

1. Erik H. Erikson, *Insight and Responsibility* (New York: W. W. Norton and Company, Inc., 1964) 112–20.
2. Gordon W. Allport, *Becoming* (New Haven: Yale University Press, 1955) 34–35.
3. Wayne E. Oates, *The Struggle to be Free* (Philadelphia: The Westminster Press, 1983) 47–48, 62–64.
4. Ibid., 48–58.
5. Ibid., 58.
6. Erik H. Erikson, *Identity: Youth and Crisis* (New York: W. W. Norton and Company, Inc., 1968) 107–14.
7. Rollo May, *Freedom and Destiny* (New York: W. W. Norton and Company, Inc., 1981) 186–87.
8. Ibid., 163–73, 185–92.
9. Maxine Schnall, *Limits: A Search for New Values* (New York: Clarkson N. Potter, Inc., 1981) 148–61, 308–09.
10. Peter Berger, "The Class Struggle in American Religion," *Moral Issues and Christian Response*, ed. Paul Jersild and Dale Johnson (New York: Holt, Rinehart and Winston, 1983) 49.
11. Rollo May, *The Courage to Create* (New York: W. W. Norton and Company, Inc., 1975) 6–11.
12. Ibid.

DISCUSSION QUESTIONS

1. What is included in a healthy form of autonomy?
2. Is it possible to have faith in God and at the same time not have a healthy form of autonomy? Explain.
3. What are examples of circumstances in the life of a college student which may tend to cause anxiety and make it difficult to act in an autonomous manner?
4. What are common examples of prejudices expressing favorable attitudes besides the ones mentioned in the chapter?
5. Describe how authoritarianism might occur in the following institutions: school, church, and business.
6. How would you describe the proper degrees of dependence and independence of young adults toward their parents?
7. What are examples of vocational and institutional norms in each of the following areas: education, health care, church, and business.
8. Considering the different types of institutions of work in our society, what part do outside participants play in their major organizational and operational decisions? Do you think they should play a bigger part in these decisions in any of these institutions.

9. Is moral courage more difficult for you to attain than social courage?
10. What are examples of some unrealistic expectations toward one's parents?

CASE STUDIES

1. Tim is a junior at a college about twenty miles from where his parents live. Over the years both Tim and his parents have been actively involved in a small church that is close to his parents' home. In the last year Tim has changed his theology considerably and no longer agrees with many of the religious ideas and practices of his parents. He has not been attending church regularly in the last few months and would like to change his membership to a church that seems to be closer in its overall approach to his own. He thinks he would feel more comfortable, have a closer identification with the people, and be more willing to be involved. However, he knows that his parents are strongly opposed to the beliefs that he now holds, and he is certain that if he were to change his membership and tell them about his new theology, then he would have serious problems in his relationship with them. He also does not want to lose the financial support that they are providing him for college. Without this support it would be difficult for him to continue. What do you think Tim should do? Should he change churches? Should he tell his parents about his new theology?

2. Sam and Jean are a young married couple without children and are both attending college. Even though Sam works part-time, they are heavily dependent upon Sam's parents to help them meet their tuition costs and other expenses. Over the last several months a problem has arisen in that Sam's parents have begun to make some new demands on them. They are insisting that Sam and Jean move closer to their own house and also are beginning to tell them how they ought to spend their money. Sam and Jean are disturbed by this behavior of Sam's parents and are considering what they should do. What do you think they should do? Should they try to discuss the problem with Sam's parents? Should they seek to become financially independent from Sam's parents?

3. Ben is a white, middle-aged employee of a utility company and is married with two children. He has a friend named Hank who has worked with him in the company for several years. Hank is also middle-aged with a wife and two children, but he is a member of a minority group. Hank was recently bypassed by the company when promotions were given, and others with less experience and training were promoted instead of him. Ben is aware that their supervisor has a deep prejudice against minorities and that this is probably responsible for Hank not being promoted. Ben has talked to the supervisor about Hank's situation and simply has been told that Hank is not deserving of another position. He wonders if he should go beyond the supervisor and talk to higher officials in the company about this matter. Ben realizes that he himself will be considered for a promotion in the near future, and he would like to avoid angering the supervisor. What do you think Ben should do?

SUGGESTIONS FOR FURTHER READING

Allport, Gordon W. *Becoming.* New Haven: Yale University Press, 1955.
Erikson, Erik H. *Identity: Youth and Crisis.* New York: W. W. Norton and Company, Inc., 1968.
_____. *Insight and Responsibility.* New York: W. W. Norton and Company, Inc., 1964.
May, Rollo. *The Courage to Create.* New York: W. W. Norton and Company, Inc., 1975.
_____. *Freedom and Destiny.* New York: W. W. Norton and Company, Inc., 1981.
Oates, Wayne E. *The Struggle to be Free.* Philadelphia: The Westminster Press, 1983.
Rogers, Carl R. *On Becoming a Person.* Boston: Houghton Mifflin Company, 1961.
Schnall, Maxine. *Limits: A Search for New Values.* New York: Clarkson N. Potter, Inc., 1981.

CHAPTER 6
LOOKING TOWARD THE FUTURE

The tension between individualism and community has been analyzed in terms of the four value conflicts of achievement and benevolence, private interests and the public good, detachment and involvement, and independence and dependence. It has been pointed out in regard to each of these that it is possible to reconcile the two different sides of the conflict. That is, in each case the two sides can be joined together into a workable position. This does not mean that these conflicts will no longer exist or that problematic questions will cease to be present in these areas. For each of these an approach can be worked out whereby the conflicts and the specific issues that arise can be consistently and constructively encountered.

Even though these basic value conflicts have been analyzed and ways of reconciling them have been set forth, it is still necessary to look more closely at the general concepts of individualism and community. Some questions about these concepts as a whole as well as dynamics concerning their relationship have not yet been addressed. Since these concepts play such a significant role in the American life-style, it is imperative that they be carefully examined. They should be understood in a variety of dimensions including the past, present, and the future. Certainly it is beneficial to know the ideas and activities associated with individualism and community in the past and present, but by itself this is not adequate. Knowledge of these concepts must also be directed toward the future in the sense that decisions must be made about how they will be approached in the years to come. That is, the question must be raised about how individualism and community should be understood and practiced. What kind of individualism and community should Americans seek in the future?

This last chapter responds to this question. It returns to a consideration of the general concepts of individualism and community and offers an explanation of how these notions should be approached in the future. It defines the meaning of a reformed individualism and genuine community and then provides practical suggestions about how these can be reached in one's individual life.

REFORMED INDIVIDUALISM

As an effort is made to focus on the category of individualism, it first should be emphasized that it has a positive side. Perhaps a more accurate assessment is to say that it has the potential for being positive. Through such qualities as autonomy and achievement, it is capable of greatly enhancing society as well as the life of the individual. However, in order for individualism to reach this potential, it must be properly viewed and applied. That is, there must be an overall approach to individualism which enables it to be used in a constructive manner. What kind of approach would this be? What kind of individualism would be able to make a high level of contribution to both society and the individual?

Several characteristics of individualism should be mentioned. One of these is the need for individualism to be responsible. Personal freedom and responsibility must be joined together. A mature and healthy life-style combines responsibility with freedom, but, as Rollo May says, this goal demands that freedom be given structure.[1] The freedom of the individual must carry with it certain guidelines including not only the laws and norms of society but also numerous self-imposed restrictions. Outward and inward regulations are both required.

Fundamental to one's inward regulations is the ability to accept certain limits in life. These limits may take a variety of forms including traffic laws, personal abilities, individual rights, bodily restrictions, and even the ultimate limit of death. Americans typically have trouble recognizing and accepting limits such as these, but a responsible type of individualism has confronted these limits and affirms them in everyday life. Along with the acceptance of limits, one must have the self-discipline to obey them. One must have the ability to discipline oneself to act in a way that may be contrary to one's subjective inclinations. The responsible person is able to carry out deeds which may be disliked and even painful. Conversely, this approach is willing to turn away from actions which may be desirable. In other words, a responsible freedom goes beyond immediate gratification to self-discipline and to act in a manner best in the long term.

When freedom is supported by a sound structure, it can be kept under control and can function properly. Without this structure freedom becomes irresponsible and is destructive for both the individual and society as a whole. Unfortunately the current structure undergirding responsible freedom in American society has to a great extent become inadequate, especially in regard to our inward regulations. This is a serious problem in American culture today, for in many ways our society's personal freedom is operating out of control. As Stanley Hauerwas says, "We have made 'freedom of the individual' an end in itself and have ignored that fact that most of us do not have the slightest idea of what we should do with our freedom."[2] Americans are granted a large amount of personal freedom in choosing their philosophy, values, and way of life, but at the same time very little instruction is provided about how to use this freedom. Many have difficulty in finding a meaningful life-style and in understanding the necessity for social laws and inward regulations. As a result, our society is increasingly threatened by a variety of irresponsible behavior such as alcoholism, drug abuse, violence, sexual promiscuity, unwed mothers and fathers, and unnecessary abortions.

What will help produce a more responsible individualism in our society? What can be done to deal with this problem? This is a broad problem with many issues related to it, but an effective way of improving the situation is by helping our youth be more responsible. It is typical for teenagers to be heavily involved in the different manifestations of this problem which points to weaknesses in their upbringing and treatment. In many ways our youth today have more freedom and receive less guidance than the youth of America's past. So often not much is expected of junior high and high school students in regard to assisting the family and contributing to the public good. It is also common for them to be extremely slow in improving their sense of self-understanding and gaining a realistic view of life. Furthermore, there are a substantial number who are severely deficient in their ability to practice certain basic human values like respect for others and self-control.

Generally speaking, many believe that American teenagers ought to be offered less freedom and at the same time be provided more teaching and direction. Three areas in which more guidance would especially be beneficial are the family, social institutions, and the legal system. Parents should show more interest in their children, spend more time with them, give them more instruction and discipline, and demand more from them in terms of responsible behavior. Additionally, our religious and educational institutions must give more attention to moral instruction and the practical questions of daily life. Churches and public schools need to allow more opportunities for different value issues to be studied and discussed in an open manner. Moreover, more legal restrictions placed on youths might benefit them and society. For example, local ordinances prohibiting young people under a certain age from being on public streets after a certain time in the evening might help prevent undesirable behavior.

Thus, it is important that individualism be responsible, but it should also be enlightened. Various types of practical knowledge often make a significant contribution toward the person being able to act in a responsible manner. American society through its norms and traditional ways of thinking and acting strongly encourages its members in the direction of certain philosophies of life. This encouragement takes the form of these outlooks being emphasized and practiced by large numbers of people in everyday life, but it also occurs through the fact that many people seldom, if ever, experience a critical examination of these outlooks or become familiar with contrary approaches. However, an enlightened individualism has a knowledge of these common American philosophies. There is an awareness not only of the limitations of these philosophies but also of the extent to which alternatives are workable and rewarding.

Several examples of these everyday philosophies could be discussed. One of these is a concept of success examined in Chapter 2 which assumes that success must be understood in terms of increasing one's wealth and status. However, an example that has not been mentioned is what can be called "the good time ethic" which thinks in terms of spending as much time as possible seeking pleasure. The phrase "a good time" is defined along the lines of experiences which are exciting, satisfying to the senses, and directly pleasurable. Experiences of this sort should be sought for their own sake, and other activities such as working and studying should be avoided whenever possible. These other activities may be necessary, but they are usually thought of as being far removed from what is pleasurable and really desirable. In most circumstances the goal is to complete them as soon as possible so that one can start having a good time. Also, this approach understands the values within individualism in a way which is consistent with this philosophy. For instance, one's private interests are especially those things which will bring about personal pleasure, and achievement is thought of as enjoyment or at least as gaining something to make pleasure possible.

An enlightened individualism recognizes that this approach makes too sharp a separation between experiences that are immediately pleasurable and other endeavors, and, consequently, it is extremely difficult to find much personal fulfillment from efforts at work or school. It also realizes that this approach in itself is highly self-centered and that a preoccupation with it easily results in feelings of alienation, guilt, and despair. Furthermore, enlightened individualism acknowledges that pleasurable experiences may sometimes include the kind of pursuits that are emphasized by this outlook, but it has a much broader concept of the experiences that are satisfying and worth seeking. It is able to include actions and relationships which are somewhat painful, which involve sacrifices for others, and which may not bring any obvious reward to oneself.

An enlightened individualism, therefore, knows about the weaknesses of these common philosophies and is able to make use of other possibilities. How is this practical knowledge achieved? Indeed to some extent it comes through the trial and error of life's events, and for many who have it this is almost entirely the way that it has been reached. However, our society leans too heavily on the idea that this knowledge must be acquired over the years through life's experiences. Certainly it is possible to teach people the nature of these philosophies and to inform them of alternatives. It would be highly beneficial if our family instruction would focus more on this area and if our religious and educational institutions would give more attention to providing people with this kind of information.

In addition to being responsible and enlightened, our individualism must also be compassionate. Several facets to the meaning of this compassion exist. First, this individualism avoids becoming so caught up in personal goals and competitive efforts that it is largely indifferent to the circumstances of others. Instead, it is keenly aware that other people also have private interests and are seeking to be autonomous and reach their own goals. Additionally, people are willing to carry out acts which help others achieve and grow, even though at times it may be at the expense of one's own advancement. This individualism feels an identification with the affairs of others and is seeking to assist them in their development.

Second, compassionate individualism acknowledges that working alone is not always the most productive or beneficial means of operating. It recognizes the value of cooperation and learns to work effectively with others to attain goals. It is able to join with others in both small group endeavors and in the tasks of large organizations. Furthermore, this individualism does not insist that this group involvement has to be in an area which protects one's own self-interests. The ability to extend personal initiative and cooperative action toward those matters which may be for the public good may go against one's own immediate situation. An example is legislators who help formulate and endorse bills which are best for the state or nation but which are opposed by a large majority of their constituents. Another example would be persons in certain vocations who work with others to discipline an incompetent or unethical colleague at the risk of subjecting themselves to possible lawsuits or vindictive actions.

Third, compassionate individualism admits the need for certain social restrictions and duties. It realizes that certain limitations and obligations may have to be placed on oneself in order to aid others and society as a whole. Therefore, it will support laws and regulations that uphold the public good, even if they cause personal sacrifice or inconvenience. For instance, even though state and local taxes have risen sharply in many areas in recent years, it may be necessary to vote in favor of new tax proposals. Also, it may be necessary to support laws which call for the strict control of the distribution of handguns or a mandatory requirement for the use of seat belts in motor vehicles.

Hence, we must affirm a reformed individualism which is responsible, enlightened, and compassionate, but in many ways these characteristics imply an additional quality of what individualism must be. For individualism truly to be responsible, enlightened, and compassionate, it must necessarily contain a strong community consciousness. People should be profoundly aware of one's interdependence with others and need for relationships. Individualism overlaps with community and is dependent upon it. In order for individualism to acquire its correct expression, it must include this community element.

M. Scott Peck points out that if individualism is to gain this community consciousness, the notion of rugged individualism must be rejected. Rugged individualism is a form of individualism that has been and continues to be highly prominent in the American culture. It emphasizes that one should be independent, have a strong character, and be complete in oneself. Indeed there is a sense in which a person needs to have individuation, power, and wholeness, but the fault of rugged individualism is that it recognizes only one side of our humanity. It does not acknowledge the other side of the self which includes our dependence, weakness, and incompleteness. It denies that we are weak and imperfect beings who need each other. Consequently, rugged individualism leads one to pretend not to have any limitations and to try to hide them from others. It also easily results in isolation and loneliness because the effort at hiding one's limitations from others often prevents one from being able to share and enter into close relationships.[3] As Peck says,

> This denial can be sustained only by pretense. Because we cannot ever be totally adequate, self-sufficient, independent beings, the ideal of rugged individualism encourages us to fake it. It encourages us to hide our weaknesses and failures. It teaches us to be utterly ashamed of our limitations. It drives us to attempt to be superwomen and supermen not only in the eyes of others but also in our own. It pushes us day in and day out to look as if we "had it all together," as if we were without needs and in total control of our lives. It relentlessly demands that we keep up appearances. It also relentlessly isolates us from each other. And it makes genuine community impossible.[4]

It is necessary, therefore, to have an individualism which incorporates a sense of community consciousness. Without this community awareness individualism does not affirm the complete meaning of the self and, consequently, is not able to gain a full sense of responsibility, enlightenment, and compassion. However, the nature of this community consciousness has not been explored. What kind of community element should this be? What exactly is the meaning of genuine community?

Genuine Community

Central to this meaning is the presence of relationships, for in genuine community there is an active involvement in relationships with others.

These relationships are not merely casual forms of interaction or simply associations that exist for an instrumental purpose. Instead, they are close relationships in which each of the participants is concerned about the welfare of the others. In other words, these are relationships which are personal and caring, and as a result, the members of the community have a sense of belonging. They feel a sense of being accepted by the other members and are at ease when they are in their presence.

Of course, relationships of this kind can find expression in a variety of forms such as marriages, family groups, friends, neighborhoods, churches, clubs, or work associations. Regardless of the form, if genuine community exists, there must be these close and loving relationships which bring about a sense of belonging. However, for these relationships to come into being and to continue to survive, there must be commitment. The members must have the ability to stay with each other in spite of hardships, disagreements, and individual weaknesses. Furthermore, these relationships also demand a willingness to share with other members. This implies a willingness to share possessions, but it especially refers to an ability to share oneself. That is, there is a capacity to open oneself to others and, therefore, to communicate more freely one's thoughts and experiences with the other members of the community.

Relationships of this nature are difficult to have in contemporary America. S. D. Gaede is correct in his assessment that modern life discourages the kind of relationships that constitute genuine community.[5] We are a busy people with jobs to do and goals to reach. Consequently, we so often want temporary relationships that will help us to accomplish our purposes or will be less restraining. The influence of rugged individualism is apparent. It is common for us to think in terms of being self-reliant and avoiding becoming too closely involved with others. As Gaede says,

> Modernity fundamentally undermines the thing we seek. The forces of modernization require relationships that are instrumental and temporary, not durable and unremitting. The forces of modernization assume that activities must be rational and purposeful, not valued for their longevity and inherent meaning. The forces of modernization encourage a perspective that is autonomous and individuated, not dependent or transcendent. In short, the needs of community are significantly at odds with the requirements of modernity.[6]

In addition to the significance of relationships, genuine community has other characteristics. One is seeking to include others. It avoids an exclusive attitude which makes a rigid separation between members and non-members. Instead, it makes an effort to establish new relationships and to add new members, not only for its own growth and enrichment but also for the sake of the possible new participants. True community is interested in the well-being of those outside the group and is not simply trying to assist and interact with its own members. Of course, some groups, such as families and relatives, are closed to outsiders, but even here when genuine community is present, there is an inclusive outlook. There is a desire to join with nonmembers in personal and caring relationships and to accept them as much as possible.

This inclusive quality of genuine community extends to all persons regardless of their particular circumstances. One barrier that can hinder this community is a narrow kind of nationalism which thinks only of what is helpful to one's own country. Robert McAfee Brown points out that in the world today it is vital that we transcend this narrow nationalism. He emphasizes that we live in a global village with a common enemy consisting of world hunger, poverty, and population growth along with the ecological crisis and the possibility of nuclear war. Problems like these are a threat to all nations, and what one country does in one of these areas may affect many countries and even the entire world. These problems have global significance and must be dealt with through a cooperative effort of many countries. Consequently, it is essential that we recognize our interdependence with the citizens of other nations and think more in terms of being a global village.[7] As Brown says,

> As we look at the world today, we can only see a world that is going to get more perplexing, complex, and threatening. . . . In a world that cannot endure extreme divisions between rich and poor, there will be increasing demands from the poor for a legitimate share of the world's resources, and increasing defensiveness on the part of the rich against inroads into what they—into what we—currently have . . . the imperative need, and the only effective counterforce for peace and justice, is surely some embodiment of global community. . . . We live in a global village and we cannot wish that fact away.[8]

Genuine community, therefore, extends to all people. It even extends to the environment. Obviously the environment cannot be involved in relationships in the same manner as human beings, but, nevertheless, a true community spirit is concerned for the welfare of the environment and is striving to have a healthy relationship with it. It seeks to cooperate with the various aspects of nature and to avoid misusing them. This kind of spirit is manifested in a number of ways such as through efforts to reduce pollution, maintain the balances within nature, prevent wasteful activities, and protect lower forms of life from exploitation and extinction.

Thus, genuine community is centered in personal and loving relationships and has an inclusive character, but it also contains the qualities of autonomy and honesty. Its members have the freedom of independent judgment and are encouraged to express themselves in an honest manner. Here is another point where the concepts of individualism and community should overlap. It has already been observed that a reformed individualism must have a strong community consciousness. Now it is being indicated that if a true form of community is present, it will contain the element of independent thinking. The concepts of individualism and community are interdependent. Each needs the presence of the other to be able to reach its highest level.

Why does genuine community need autonomy and honesty? They make possible an open atmosphere in which people are more relaxed and more willing to be themselves. People show a greater willingness to let their true selves come forth and to share themselves with others. Without these qualities pretense and an absence of effective communication prevail. Also, autonomy and honesty stimulate personal growth and group efficiency. They facilitate the process by which group members are able to gain from the knowledge and experience of others, and when group tasks and goals exist, they make it easier for members to offer their particular contributions to these endeavors.

Americans should have group experiences of autonomy and honesty, but unfortunately, as M. Scott Peck points out, our community efforts frequently lead only to the presence of pseudocommunity which results in a denial of autonomy and honesty. Peck describes pseudocommunity as being essentially a group which minimizes or ignores individual differences. In order to avoid conflicts, the members pretend to have the same beliefs and values, regardless of whether they actually do or not. Rather than learning to deal with conflicts as in true community, pseudocommunity simply tries to prevent them from being expressed. Every effort must be made to avoid outward disagreements or any statement or action which would offend someone. Moreover, pseudocommunities are characterized by generalities. Members tend to set forth their ideas in broad terms without attempting to be precise or to offer explanations. In this way, the group can more easily maintain the pretension of harmony and avoid disputes.[9]

Along with the qualities of genuine community that have already been set forth, theologians contend that community includes the presence of the Divine. This Divine involvement in genuine community occurs in several ways with one being his presence through the different characteristics of this community. God affirms such qualities as close and caring relationships, the acceptance of others, and an autonomous and honest social environment. His spirit is present through these qualities, and he wants group activities to contain them. Undoubtedly their presence in group behavior indicates that there is a sense in which the Divine is present.

Many believe God is also involved in genuine community by constantly encouraging us to accept it. He wants people to be a part of this kind of community, and he is constantly working with individual attitudes and circumstances to guide them in this direction. He not only tries to show us the value of genuine community but also seeks to persuade us to participate in it. There are numerous ways that this encouragement may take place. One example is that he may work through the loneliness and despair people may experience as a result of being alienated from others and help them to see the need for close and loving relationships. Another example is that God may be able to persuade us through the inadequacy of a pseudocommunity. People may find the experience of a pseudocommunity to be frustrating or simply unrewarding, and, therefore, they may be led to search for something that is more meaningful. A further example is that God may work in a positive way through an encounter with genuine community. A person may find an experience with a true form of community so fulfilling that there is a desire to continue in it and perhaps seek to participate in other groups of this nature.

Another way that the Divine is involved in genuine community is that he is seeking to encourage us to acknowledge his presence in this community and to become close to him. That is, along with our participation in this kind of community, he seeks to persuade us to recognize the Divine element within it and to develop a personal relationship with him. There is definitely a sense in which involvement in genuine community is at the same time to be in relationship with God. But God wants us to have a comprehensive experience with him that includes all of our relationships with others, not just those within the groups to which we belong. Additionally, he wants us to be able to follow his leadership. He wants us to be able to cooperate with his purposes and assist in carrying them out, both within our groups and in other activities. In order for this to be accomplished, we must enter into a personal and faithful association with him.

In summary, a reformed individualism is responsible, enlightened, and compassionate, and genuine community contains personal and loving relationships, has an inclusive character, allows for an autonomous and honest atmosphere, and includes the Divine. It is also the case that these forms of individualism and community are intertwined with each other. Each to some extent needs the other in order to acquire its correct expression.

SEEKING A REFORMED INDIVIDUALISM AND GENUINE COMMUNITY

As we look toward the future, there is still the question of how this individualism and community is to be established in one's own life. What exactly can a person do in order to achieve this type of individualism and community? There are a number of constructive suggestions that can be offered.

1. *Strive to control greed and envy.* Chapter 3 pointed out the need to discourage greed and envy, but further attention to these is now necessary because of the overall effect of these qualities on individualism and community. Greed and envy receive a large amount of encouragement within American society, especially in the area of acquiring a higher standard of living. Americans are expected to want more of a variety of possessions and experiences and to want at least as much as their friends and neighbors have. However, a reformed individualism and genuine community cannot be attained when greed and envy are allowed to operate with little or no restraint. These qualities easily interfere with a responsible, enlightened and compassionate life-style, and they also can create barriers that prevent close associations with others.

It should be acknowledged, as Erich Fromm indicates, that the strength of greed and envy within American society does not result from a fact of nature but rather from a cultural impetus.[10] It may be that to some extent these qualities are inherent within human nature, but the large degree which they are found in American society is definitely not inherent. There is a well established social factor operating which gives approval to these values, and this means that it is not inevitable that an individual give them the emphasis that they often receive. It is possible for a person to bring greed and envy under control and to keep them from exercising their destructive potential. Of course, this demands that the individual recognize the negative possibilities of greed and envy and also be able to cope with the social pressure to accept them.

2. *Promote practical instruction.* Our society has often been deficient in providing direction to its members about everyday values and philosophies of life. As previously indicated, there is a need for more emphasis in this regard in both family life and the various institutions in society. Usually this instruction should be offered in an open atmosphere in which those involved are encouraged to reflect and think for themselves. Undoubtedly there are situations, especially within the family, when instruction must be offered in an authoritative and forceful manner, but this approach should be avoided as much as possible. Instead of dictating ideas to others, it is much more beneficial for them to have the opportunity to ask questions, compare different views, and make their own decisions.

Sometimes instruction about these practical issues of life has been given through the example of the way a person lives. This can be a productive method, but it has not been uncommon for it to be used as an excuse for not having to do anything else. So often the method of personal example is more effective when it is joined with discussion and explanations. By itself, it is subject to being misunderstood and does not provide the opportunity for examining other approaches.

3. *Affirm guidelines which are supported by self-discipline.* The right kind of individualism demands that a person be organized in terms of some fundamental principles. These values should serve as a basis for decisions and actions and should be carefully examined before being adopted. Ideally the person should go through a process of analyzing many different possible values and become deeply convinced of the guidelines that are finally adopted. These principles also must be supported by an emphasis upon personal discipline which implies the ability to force oneself to do something when it is undesirable or unpleasant in the immediate sense. When this self-control is present, the individual has a greater ability to remain loyal to personal guidelines even under difficult circumstances.

Along with self-discipline, an effort must be made to aid others, particularly young people, to move in this direction. One must be willing to interact with others and assist them in constructing their own guidelines. It also is frequently necessary to help others acquire a sense of self-discipline. This may take the form of persuading others, or at times in some way forcing them, to carry out actions that they consider unpleasant or simply do not want to do. In some siutations, such as within families, it may also require that certain punishments be levied if assigned tasks are not performed.

4. *Seek to be more tolerant and open toward others.* Tolerance and openness are qualities which greatly facilitate genuine community. Tolerance does not insist that agreement must always be present or that everybody must like each other. It understands that there may sometimes be conflicts and negative feelings, but it has the capacity to affirm others in spite of these differences. When tolerance is present, there is the ability in all circumstances to recognize others as individuals deserving communication and consideration. Consequently, there is the willingness to allow others to speak and to listen to what they say. There is also the willingness to reach out to others in the form of conversation or some type of mutual activity.

Openness goes along with tolerance and demands that one be able to share oneself with others, although it is recognized that everyone has certain things that should remain private. It is indeed possible to disclose too much of oneself as well as not enough. However, in our society the tendency is usually in the direction of not revealing enough of who we are instead of revealing too much. In most cases we need to be willing to show more of ourselves to others including both our present interests and concerns and our past experiences and failures.

5. *Think of relationships as a vital part of life.* As already indicated, it is easy in our society to think of relationships as secondary occurrences. However,

it is important for the correct expression of both individualism and community that relationships be regarded as an essential part of one's life. This has reference to all types of interaction with others, but it especially applies to our associations with friends, family members, and other relatives. These close associations must be taken seriously and given a high priority in our decisions and behavior, meaning that adequate time will be devoted to them and that efforts will be made to ensure that they are rewarding. These experiences with our close associates should be ones that are thought of with anticipation and which bring a large amount of joy and fulfillment to our lives.

6. *Look for community in a variety of places.* Certainly we should expect to find community with our close associates, but, as Thomas Bender points out, we cannot expect to have community with everyone.[11] All of us will have contact with many people and groups in which community is not a realistic possibility and, therefore, the experience of community has to be a limited part of our lives. Nevertheless, sometimes community may emerge in some facet of our lives when we are not expecting it and are unable to take advantage of the opportunity. Thus, we must learn to look for community in a variety of places such as in churches, classes, clubs, civic endeavors, music groups, business ventures, and athletic activities. One place that the potential for community is sometimes overlooked is the work environment. A person's work involvement frequently offers one the chance to get to know new people and to develop some close relationships.

7. *Be willing to work at having community.* The presence of community is not always an experience that comes naturally or easily. So often it is something that has to be worked at and mastered, and this usually applies not only to bringing it into existence but also to maintaining it. One must be willing to put forth an effort in order to initiate friendships and community. It also means that one must be willing to remain in relationships with others even when they involve hardships, conflicts, embarrassments, or disappointments. For instance, one should seek to continue relationships with friends in spite of unfair treatment or should choose to stay within a church or club even though there are weaknesses and disagreements.

8. *Become interested in something beyond oneself.* A preoccupation with activities and goals which are merely for personal gratification serves as a firm obstacle to having a reformed individualism and being able to participate in genuine community. In particular it hinders the growth and operation of compassionate behavior and close relationships. Therefore, it is necessary for one to become dedicated to something which is not predominantly promoting oneself, such as perhaps getting involved in a social issue, a political movement, a civic concern, a religious activity, a leadership role in a youth group, or even a task in a foreign country. This kind of involvement

can provide a chance for a person to go beyond a narrow self-concern and to develop a healthy personal attitude. At the same time, it also can offer some valuable opportunities for experiences of community.

9. *Give God more of an opportunity to work.* Joined with each of these previous suggestions is the need for God's help in reaching a reformed individualism and genuine community. While attempting to implement all of these other suggestions, one should also maintain a personal relationship to the Divine through such practices as prayer, meditation, and worship. This gives God more of an opportunity to work in one's life in the sense that the individual has the kind of outlook that is receptive to Divine guidance. Through a Divine relationship an individual becomes open to the assistance that God offers for reaching this kind of individualism and community.

NOTES

1. Rollo May, *Man's Search for Himself* (New York: W. W. Norton and Company, 1953) 165–73.
2. Stanley Hauerwas, *A Community of Character* (Notre Dame, Indiana: University of Notre Dame Press, 1981) 80.
3. M. Scott Peck, *The Different Drum* (New York: Simon and Schuster, 1987) 56–58.
4. Ibid., 56–57.
5. S. D. Gaede, *Belonging* (Grand Rapids: Zondervan Publishing House, 1985) 46–47.
6. Ibid.
7. Robert McAfee Brown, *Making Peace in the Global Village* (Philadelphia: The Westminster Press, 1981) 93–104.
8. Ibid., 103–04.
9. Peck, 86–90.
10. Erich Fromm, *To Have or To Be?* (New York: Bantam Books, 1976) 184.
11. Thomas Bender, *Community and Social Change in America* (New Brunswick, New Jersey: Rutgers University Press, 1978) 143–50.

DISCUSSION QUESTIONS

1. What changes within society would you suggest for helping American teenagers be more responsible?
2. Do you think that "the good time ethic" is a popular philosophy in our society? What do you think should be done to assist people in becoming more aware of the weaknesses of a philosophy such as this?
3. What is rugged individualism? Do you think that it is more commonly practiced by males than females in our society?
4. What factors in American society would you mention which sometimes make it difficult to have close and caring relationships with others?
5. What is the difference between the right kind of loyalty to one's country and a narrow nationalism? What are some examples of the way narrow nationalism expresses itself?
6. What is a pseudocommunity? Are you able to give an example of a pseudocommunity with which you have been associated? Why would you say it was a pseudocommunity?

7. Do people in some sense have a relationship with God when they practice qualities which God supports and encourages?

8. Are you aware of any characteristics of our society which make it difficult to practice self-discipline?

9. What is the difference between liking others and loving them? Is it possible to love others but not like them?

10. What are reasons that genuine community is not a realistic possibility in some of our contacts with people?

SUGGESTIONS FOR FURTHER READING

Bender, Thomas. *Community and Social Change in America.* New Brunswick, New Jersey: Rutgers University Press, 1978.

Brown, Robert McAfee. *Making Peace in the Global Village.* Philadelphia: The Westminster Press, 1981.

Hauerwas, Stanley. *A Community of Character.* Notre Dame, Indiana: University of Notre Dame Press, 1981.

Kamenka, Eugene, ed. *Community as a Social Ideal.* New York: St. Martin's Press, 1982.

Kirkpatrick, Frank G. *Community: A Trinity of Models.* Washington: Georgetown University Press, 1986.

May, Rollo. *Man's Search for Himself.* New York: W. W. Norton and Company, 1953.

Peck, M. Scott. *The Different Drum.* New York: Simon and Schuster, 1987.

INDEX